THE INFLUENCE OF MILITARY STRATEGIES TO BUSINESS

SKILLS TO HELP WITH PROBLEM SOLVING & DECISION MAKING

M.D. WHITE

Dedicated to my greatest achievement, my most prized possession

MONTE

Cover design by Katie Norton

Layout and interior design by Ashley Clarke at All Stories Editing

Printed in the United States of America

First Printing, 2017 Second Printing 2018

HOPEFUL MEDIA SOLUTIONS LLC

845 East Highway 88, Suite 247 Jackson, CA. 95642
www.HopefulMediaSolutions.com

ISBN-13: 978-1-947920-02-6

INTRODUCTION

The parallels between war and business planning are numerous. The important distinctions between war and business planning involve the ultimate ends of a given conflict. War involves physical destruction and death. When a business conducts operations, economic utility is generated, and employees, stakeholders, and society on the whole derive some benefit. The nature of competition is generally regulated by law, and if disputes arise among rivals, either marketplace conditions or legal systems will make a binding decision over corporate life and death, victory or defeat. Introducing the analogies of war into the business environment is complex and may arouse emotions and an ethos contrary to the culture of commerce. As multinational businesses expand their reach, they can be engines of wealth generation and peace. However, if global corporations adopt an overly martial ideology, then the hopes for human progress and cultural evolution will be dashed.

WAR PLANNING

The fundamental objective of a war plan is the imposition of the victor's terms on the opponent, which could also be defined as total victory. Military historians can cite exclusions to this definition, however, the purpose of this book is not centered on arcane military history debates. With few exceptions, modern military conflict results in the deaths of the combatants' armed forces and civilians, and the physical destruction of property and economic assets. Additionally, war plans are usually carefully planned before a conflict but are rarely executed exactly as projected during the engagement. The arrangements are generally redeveloped in lieu of alterations during a war.

An example of grand strategy conflict was the Pacific campaign waged between Japan and America from 1941 to1945. Prior to engaging America and Great Britain in 1941, the Japanese created a detailed stratagem. It was designed to suddenly destroy the offensive capabilities of both the Americans (the Pacific fleet at Pearl Harbor) and the British (key military bases in Singapore and Hong Kong), the rapid seizure of economic resources and territories in Southeast

Asia (present-day Malaysia and Indonesia) and the Western Pacific (the Philippines, Guam, Wake and Midway Islands). The Japanese planned to achieve these objectives within six months of the start of hostilities. The ultimate goal of the Japanese was to rampage in Southeast Asia and the Pacific, then propose a peace settlement with a demoralized America and Britain to gain international recognition of the Empire of Japan as a superpower.

America had anticipated war with Japan since the late 1800s and crafted and periodically revised many offensive strategies culminating in "War Plan Orange." It served as the United States' Pacific war plan until the defeat of Japan in September 1945. Plan Orange called for a decisive naval engagement with the Japanese off the coast of the Philippines, then a naval blockade of the Japanese home islands to force Japan's surrender. Events (successful air and naval campaigns) and new technology (the submarine, aircraft carrier, and atomic bomb) and other tactical considerations altered Plan Orange, however its strategic goal of imposing America's will on Japan was achieved.

Many military historians and contemporary business students view the **Chinese military strategist, Sun Tzu (ca.500 B.C.E.) as the developer of the Bible of strategy**. Wong, Maher, and Lee (1998) confirmed that Sun Tzu's principles are divided into basically two components:

1. **Knowing oneself**
2. **Knowing the enemy**

Although Sun Tzu recommended that war be avoided if at all possible, he provided warriors with the principles of strategy if war erupted. Many of Tzu's teachings have laid the foundation for today's theory of strategic management. Sun Tzu's strategy consisted of five elements:

- Tao
- Weather
- Terrain
- Leadership
- Systems

These elements are presently thought of in terms of external and internal environmental analysis in present-day strategic management. Sun Tzu believed that close management and monitoring of the five factors would build a strong organization.

Sun Tzu's five elements constitute the basic components that comprise any war plan. The fundamentals of war planning which includes an assessment of one's capabilities and gathering intelligence on the enemy to determine their strengths, weaknesses, capabilities, and intentions. However, the most important goal of any war plan is victory over the adversary. War involves deploying as many factors necessary to achieve triumph, including the sacrifice of human lives and consuming as many physical (oil, metals, food) and economic (production plans, currency controls, etc.) assets as required to accomplish the objective.

Finally, war involves great risk. One side, such as Japan, can initiate a conflict to achieve results. However, if the instigator is unsuccessful, it may lose control over its destiny and physical territory and be subject to physical occupation by the victor.

This book focuses on and is filled with tracts touting the adaptations of military strategy and other analogies to guide businesses. Most researchers, for example, point out how the military doctrine of C3I (command, control, communication, and information) which should be the basis for corporations to manage crises. The author studied three contamination cases faced by Perrier, Vita Soy, and Coca-Cola, as examples of how large corporations used C3I to effectively deal with a clear and present danger. Most researchers have enthusiastically embraced the corporate use of military doctrine.

Reflecting the spirit of the times, they have promoted the exploration of a deterrence strategy "because if properly devised and executed, deterrent strategies offer the highest return and help to preserve intact the company's security, sovereignty, and power." The researcher's entire presentation is laced with Cold War terminology.

They sound like a President's national security advisor when they proclaim that the four key elements of a successful corporate deterrence strategy are:

- Credibility
- Capability
- Communication
- Rationality

After reading the above, one can almost imagine a McDonald's executive putting all of its stores on "red alert" status and scrambling its franchises to be prepared to launch a preemptive soft serve ice cream sale on Wendy's.

Some other researchers take lessons from a classic Indian epic the Bhagavad Gita, to derive management strategies. The Bhagavad Gita stresses "self-control focusing on discipline in perseverance, detachment from fruits of labor, and devotion to duty. The key components in business management are the 5Cs:

- Capital
- Capability
- Connections
- Communication
- Commitment

While the analogies between war and business planning may

feel superficial and appear transferable, some researchers argue against not only the overt comparisons but describe the subtle damage that a military lexicon may have on businesses. The research shows that post-industrial business is less rigid and command-control oriented, requiring less hierarchical structures and more independence, creative employees.

Present day leaders should have softer leadership styles because followers are less likely to tolerate orders barked at them. Even the use of martial language "remains seductive and damaging, as it subconsciously appeals to the inherent and timeless aggressive human instincts aimed at confrontation which are hidden beyond a thin veneer of civilized behavior and convention."

The reverse analogy (business terminology used by the military) would also seem inappropriate. Frequently the military utilizes corporate terms to sanitize the reality of warfare. For example, many military briefings use the term "collateral damage" to mean civilians were killed and residential buildings were destroyed. Nuclear and chemical/biological weapons are expressed as weapons of mass destruction. Researchers have talked to individuals who have worked in the Pentagon describing an aircraft crash as "a negative interface with the environment." When warfare is reduced to a corporate-like discussion of the return on investment, the true cost of conflict is minimized or missed.

True warriors wish to avoid war. Armchair generals considering waging war viewed in corporate terms may be tempted to venture into conflict believing that if the "investment" does not deliver sufficient returns, one can just "write it off" like a bad stock investment.

BUSINESS PLANNING

After considering the above military and literary guides to developing strategies, researchers have become cynical about looking at alternative realities for strategic guidance. They have defined strategy as "the major courses of action (choices) selected and implemented to achieve one or more goals." This concise definition serves as an introduction to a variety of strategic planning options that have emerged over the past several decades.

In *The Art and Process of Strategy Development and Deployment* (2005) nine strategic models are offered that seemingly gather the best approaches the civilian world offers.

The Harvard Business Model defines strategy as a pattern of purposes and policies defining the company and its business.

Strategic Planning Systems is a systematic approach that makes it possible for managers to make, implement, and control decisions across the organization Strategic Management is the bridge between the organization and its stakeholders

Portfolio Method, which analyzes the prevailing market conditions for the specific business category Competitive Analysis studies the forces that shape an industry from a profitability perspective

Strategic Issues Management focuses attention on the recognition and resolution of strategic issues

Strategic Negotiations view strategy as the partial resolution of organizational issues through a highly political process The Framework for Innovation emphasizes the development of innovative strategies that promote creativity and entrepreneurship at a local level Logical Incrementalism that focuses on appropriately balancing an overall direction for the organization with centralized decision-making

The nine strategies outlined above reveal a great deal about the process to devise a strategy. However, the question remains, regardless of the method one uses to produce a strategy, what makes one notable? Some researchers have taken a different approach to evaluating strategy creation. They argue that a shift must occur away from teaching and practicing of the process of strategic planning to one centered on the criteria for evaluating them and emphasizing the importance of tactics in implementation.

Researchers also consider the discussion regarding which strategic planning analogy, methodology, or process consistently produces a winning formula. Their assertion that learners and professionals should use historical lessons not as recipes but rather as opportunities to recognize brilliant thinking makes great sense and merits immediate attention. In today's "me too, but cheaper" culture of commerce, it is believed that grafting or imitating a successful strategy is a prescription for success. The difficulty in imitating is deciding what should be copied.

Many motorcycle manufacturers have tried to imitate the Harley-Davidson motorcycle. Most have focused on copying the physical product, including the sound of the motor. However, the unique characteristics of Harley-Davidson products cannot be captured in three-dimensional objects. Harley's appeal is in its mystique of rugged independence and shared owner/driver identity. Like the Harley, corporate strategy must define a matchless plan and process to implement and sustain competitive advantage.

COMPARISONS AND CONTRASTS
BETWEEN WAR AND BUSINESS

The determination by a firm as to how it assesses its competitive position relative to the industry it competes in, its competition, forces in the industry, and future trends are generic considerations for both military and civilian applications.

When comparing war and business planning, several similarities are evident. Plans are devised to achieve victory. The definition of victory may be relative. In the military, triumph may mean imposing one nation-state's will on another, the physical seizure of certain foreign assets, deterring attack, or mounting an active defense to secure the borders of a nation/state. In the business world, success may be the acquisition of a competitor, seizure of a targeted market, prevention of market share loss, or the defense of proprietary technology.

One of the most valuable assets that the military and businesses covet is intelligence on their opponents.

War inevitably involves taking lives, the destruction of property and environmental degradation and expending expensive equipment. Most enlightened generals urge their leaders to avoid the horrors of war, risk of defeat and destruction and to seek other means to accomplish national goals.

The nature of free enterprise is taking risk. Boards of directors, greedy stockholders and other forces push corporate leaders into jeopardy.

Enterprises can engage in high-risk competition to benefit their "citizens" (stakeholders) and community at large without the massive physical dislocation caused by armed conflict.

When a company "loses" to a major competitor, the landscape is not littered with death, destruction, and degradation.

Although employees may need to find other employment, stockholders may lose their investment capital, and communities experience the negative effects of job and tax losses, all parties live to try again.

It is vital that business students, corporate leaders, and military theorists recognize the natural borders of one another's "areas of operations." Using a mistaken strategic analogy equals hiring an attorney to provide medical services.

Essential internal and external environmental factors

We define strategic planning as diagnosing the organization's external and internal environments, deciding on a vision and mission, developing overall goals, creating and selecting general strategies to be pursed and allocating resources to achieve the organization's goals. Many scholars have made pronouncements on what are critical internal and external environmental forces. Many researchers place the environmental analysis as the second and third steps of their strategic planning model, after the creation of the vision, mission, and values. They note that a variety of variables affect the evaluation of a firm's organic assets and liabilities including competitors, new entrants, customers, suppliers, and substitution possibilities.

Most researchers state that the rivalry among existing competitors varies depending on how management views its rivals. The threat of new entrants is generally in reaction to high profits earned by an established firm or rapid growth in the industry. The bargaining power of customers relies on their ability to pit one company against another to force prices down, increase higher quality, and obtain more products/services for the same price (bundling packages, including exclusive vacations, value meals and etc.).

The bargaining power of suppliers enlarges when they can raise or protect market share, boost prices, or eradicate some features without worrying about losing customers. The threat of substitute products or services depends on consumers' willingness to alter their buying habits, for example changing traditional landline telephone service to cellular phone service.

Most researchers assess an entity's strengths and weaknesses to identify the company's core competencies and select which ones need to be improved. An organization's core competencies "are the strengths that make the organization distinctive and competitiveness by providing goods or services that are of unique value to its customers" Core competencies are sorted out into these general categories:

- Superior
- Technological capability
- Reliable processes
- Close relationships with external shareholders

Among the diagnostic factors are market share, technology capacity, human resources, new product development, fiscal viability, managerial suitability, and brand reputation. Many researchers' internal and external analysis process is a sophisticated update of Sun Tzu's dictum about never fearing the outcome of one thousand battles if one knows themselves and their opponents.

Some other researchers segment the environment into two components, remote and operating. The firm's external environment consists of economic, social, political, technological and ecological factors. Those forces that directly affect the enterprise (internal or operating environment) include the industry in which it competes, its competitive position, customer profiles, suppliers, creditors, and the labor market. They also affirm that the purpose of the external analysis is to identify strategic opportunities and threats in an organization's operating environment and how they will affect the company's mission. An internal analysis locates the strengths and weaknesses of the firm.

The researchers above allude to Porter's Five Force Model of industry competition.

The five forces are the threat of new entrants, the bargaining power of buyers, the bargaining power of suppliers, the threat of substitutes, and the intensity of the rivalry of industry competitors. Analyzing these five forces according to Porter is an essential tool for assessing the impact that environmental forces have on the business. Porter's Five Force Model is not an unassailable strategic planning instrument.

If an industry's structure completely decided how all the firms in that sector conducted business there would be no differentiation. For example, since all competitors in the ketchup industry use fundamentally the same ingredients, everyone in the business should follow the same pricing strategy. Alternatively, if all companies in ketchup commerce have the same unit cost profitability, the variation between these adversaries could be attributed to random events.

In reality, all competition is not equal. Competitors differ in how they are organized, structured and how they present their products. The differentiation includes marketing practices, fiscal and operating conditions, and operating techniques. Such distinctions may also be attributed to variations in market intelligence.

A crucial capability for both military and civilian planning is access to market information or, put in the military parlance, intelligence. As noted by McManus and Botten (2006), an organization can diligently and precisely follow one of the many chic strategic planning models that are available and still fail, because it did not conduct "strategic surveillance." It should monitor a broad range of events inside and outside the corporation likely to impact the implementation of its strategy.

Predicting the future is thought to be the realm of mystics. However, Hines (2006) a futurist, states that most business analysts have little experience or formal training in strategic foresight. Hines lists six phases to crafting strategic foresight.

- Framing
- Scanning
- Forecasting
- Visioning
- Planning
- Acting

Some other researchers have offered six steps to guiding corporate surveillance activities.

Sensitization to challenge the firm's existing assumptions about particular competitors

Benchmarking to compare the firm with its competitors Legitimization to justify certain proposals and persuade the firm's leaders of the feasibility and desirability of a chosen course of action

Inspiration to solve problems in this process by identifying what other firms had done in similar circumstances Planning by gathering information about others to assist the formal planning process

Decision-making to aid the operational and tactical decision-making by managers

Another vital micro factor that determines the success or failure of a strategy is the quality of the organization's chief executive officer. Hellreigel et al. (2005) define transformational leaders as having the ability to "inspire others with their vision, often promote this vision over opposition, and demonstrate confidence in themselves and their views" Transformational leadership is more than being a big picture dreamer. A transformational leader creates a vision of what the enterprise or cause can be and attracts others to the mission.

Many other researchers maintain that an organization can fail despite having a superb strategy and brilliant implementation steps.

The reasons include the leadership

1. selecting the wrong strategy
2. implementing the chosen strategy poorly
3. ignoring the strategy to concentrate on tactics.

For example, Southwest Airlines' brilliant triumph in executing its low-cost business model would be inconceivable without the transformational leadership of former CEO Herb Kelleher.

Southwest's model is straightforward in concept, however, leading and consistently executing Southwest's mission and shaping its culture were as crucial to its success as General Norman Schwarzkopf's leadership during Desert Shield/Storm.

Both Kelleher and Schwarzkopf were icons of their organizations' missions. When one considers Kelleher's and Schwarzkopf's opponents, who by most accounts were more powerful, it is amazing that both succeeded against such formidable foes. However, their leadership, personal strength of character, strategy selection, nearly flawless tactical execution and, most importantly, mastery of strategic surveillance gave them the decisive edge for recording victories.

The average lifespan of a major corporation isn't very long. If current trends hold, only one-quarter of today's S&P 500 companies will be part of the index by 2020, and the other three-quarters probably don't even exist yet.

In today's turbulent markets, companies that were once dominant are struggling to survive, and managers are constantly probing to understand what makes the difference between success and failure. Looking at today's companies, for example, we might ask why the market capitalization of Southwest Airlines is greater than that of United, American, Delta, and Northwest Airlines combined. Why is GM's Saturn subsidiary successful while its Oldsmobile unit is being put out of business? Why are FedEx, Charles Schwab, and Home Depot widely admired while Web van, At Home, and Netscape are gone, and Enron, WorldCom, Xerox, and apparently quite a few others resorted to falsified accounting to preserve the illusion of success when failure loomed?

There's a story behind each of these successes and failures. Sometimes it's a story of a great idea, sometimes it's one that failed. Sometimes it's a story of insightful management, or management that failed. But almost always, it's a story about change. Change in the market, change in the economy, change in a particular product or service that transformed a failure into a success, or vice versa.

While we study the stories to learn about the specific changes, events, insights, and breakdowns in each case, we also look for broader and deeper explanations that show how change applies across industries and the whole of the economy.

The broader patterns are the subject of this book. Here we propose a specific model explaining how large companies create and sustain market leadership and examine the traps they fall into that prevent them from doing so.

BUSINESS MODEL WARFARE

THE MORTALITY OF COMPANIES

The capacity of organizations to adapt to rapid and unexpected change has been frequently discussed but managing for adaptability is a little understood and poorly practiced art even as the pace of change continues to accelerate. In reality, more big companies are going out of business faster than ever before.

In searching for hard data about company mortality, we found three sources:

- The Fortune 500 list
- The Forbes 100 list and the S&P 500 list
- The Fortune 500

Most researchers have studied the Fortune 500 list since it was first created in 1955 and continuing through 2001 to identify the companies on the list one year, but not the subsequent year. These are the living examples of what we might call the relentless progression of competition. We found that over this span of forty-six years, an average of thirty companies per year left the list. In some years there were more departures, in some years fewer, but the overall trend showed consistent turnover of about 6% each year.

If the impact of decay was random among companies, then over a period of only about seventeen years the entire list would turn over and an entirely new set of companies would be listed. But, of course, it doesn't happen that way. Instead, some companies are ephemeral visitors to the Fortune 500, while others endure for decades. A study by planners at Shell found that by 1983, one-third of the companies listed among the 500 in 1970 had not only fallen from the list but had closed altogether. That's an average mortality rate of twelve companies per year or one per month. They also found that a multi-national corporation comparable in size to a Fortune 500 company could only be expected to survive for between forty and fifty years.

The Forbes 100

In 1917, Forbes magazine created its own list of the largest one hundred US companies. By 1987, sixty-one of those companies no longer existed. Over the seventy-year span, in other words, an average of about one company per year disappeared, of the remaining thirty-nine original companies, eighteen were still large enough to remain on the list in 1987.

However, of those eighteen companies, only two had performed better than the overall stock market during the seventy-year period. While the combined annual growth rate (CAGR) of US public companies from 1917 to 1987 was 7.5%, the eighteen surviving companies managed a combined average of only 5.3%. An investor in market index funds would have done substantially better than an investor in these eighteen companies. (This assumes that any investor would have had the incredible foresight to pick the eighteen surviving big companies from the original list of 100.)

The S&P 500

The S&P 500 list provides a third reference point. In 1957, the

S&P listing of ninety top companies was expanded to five hundred. By 1997, only seventy-four of the original five hundred companies remained, an average mortality rate of more than ten per year.

But a more detailed analysis shows that the rate of mortality has been steadily increasing, with far more companies failing as the end of the century approached. The average lifespan of an S&P 500 company has steadily decreased from more than fifty years to fewer than twenty-five today. These three slices of history convey a clear pattern. Projecting the pattern forward as we noted above, it's likely that about a third of today's major corporations will survive as significant businesses for the next twenty-five years.

"Most will die or be bought out and absorbed because they are too slow to keep pace with change in the market. By 2020, more than three-quarters of the S&P 500 will consist of companies that we don't know today." This trend in corporate mortality is a serious issue with significant implications.

THE SECOND PART

IT'S THE BUSINESS MODEL

T he context of business strategy is the marketplace in which it
plays out, so discussions of strategy must begin with reference to the market. Today, the three most critical market factors are
accelerating change, increasing competition, and increasing
complexity. While each force presents its own particular problems,
the impact of all three acting together significantly compounds the
problem, composing a "change conspiracy" that poses far greater
challenges. The results are a drastically compressed planning
horizon for every company and the need for faster responses
throughout the organization.

These conditions are taking a heavy toll on companies, industries, and entire nations, and bringing severe stress to the business
leaders who grapple with these issues day after day. On the news,
you'll hear a long list of struggling enterprises, notable not only for
the steep slide that many have recently endured but also because it
was not so long ago that they were held in high esteem. Among
them are Vivendi, United Airlines, K-mart, Xerox, WorldCom,

Tyco, Arthur Andersen, USAir, AOL Time Warner, Adelphia, Xerox, HealthSouth, Qwest, and many others.

While these companies struggle to right themselves, Argentina, Brazil, and their South American neighbors struggle to keep their economies viable in the new and demanding framework of global markets, while Japan struggles with a bout of deflation that has already lasted a decade.

Meanwhile, other companies fall more slowly. For example, steel industry icon Bethlehem Steel, once a member of the elite Dow Jones index, was recently delisted from the New York Stock Exchange when its stock value fell below one dollar per share, GM is dropping the Oldsmobile brand due to its declining market share. Another example is Sears, which dropped its own catalog some years ago, only to then buy Lands' End.

The company is also trying to sell its profitable financial services unit to raise cash to buttress its faltering retail unit.

These failures make dramatic stories illustrated by the sad losses suffered by individuals and families struggling to survive the economic losses and emotional strain. As more companies fail, it is slowly becoming clear these are no longer unusual events.

Despite the attempts by governments, central banks, and multilateral organizations such as the UN, WTO, and the World Bank to reduce the impacts of change, it's clear that the forces of change are far stronger than ever before.

BUSINESS MODEL WARFARE

T urbulence continues to increase, which means that business failures will continue to be common occurrences going forward, forcing managers to wonder obsessively deep into the night, *What should my company be doing differently?*

Creative Destruction

While the sense of crisis and the time compression caused by the change conspiracy is certainly real, the underlying dynamics of the competitive marketplace are not new. Sixty years ago, economist Joseph Schumpeter described the overall capitalist process as "creative destruction," and he pointed out that the natural behavior of capitalist systems brings revolution, not as the result of vague external factors, but from within. Change, Schumpeter observed, is the common condition, not stability. In a prescient comment about prevalent management practices at the time (and still today), he wrote, "The problem that is usually being visualized is how capitalism administers existing structures, whereas the relevant problem is how it creates and destroys them."

The significance of this comment is nearly impossible to overstate. While so many observers and managers focus their attention on how businesses perform in today's markets, Schumpeter points out that it is in the very nature of market evolution to weaken some companies while creating opportunities for others.

The parallels between war and business planning are numerous and well documented. The chief similarities between business and war planning include:

- Understanding the nature of conflict
- Comprehension of the opponent's intentions
- Knowledge of one's capabilities and deficits and that of the challenger
- Awareness of the battleground
- Ability to shape a coherent and executable strategy
- Mastery of logistics
- Belief in the righteousness of one's cause
- Intimate connection with one's suppliers, customers, and staff
- Conviction to win the battle

The important distinctions between war and business planning involve the ultimate ends of a given conflict. War involves physical destruction and death. Businesses thankfully never have to calculate their "wars" in lives lost or wounded. The great Coke/Pepsi war never destroys bottling plants, employees, or illegal espionage. In fact, Pepsi reported to Coke an effort to sell Coke's formula to Pepsi by a Coke employee.

When a business conducts operations, economic utility is generated and employees, stakeholders, and society, on the whole, derive some benefit. The nature of competition is generally regulated by law, and if disputes arise among rivals, either marketplace conditions or legal systems will make a binding decision over corporate life and death, victory or defeat.

Introducing the analogies of war into the business environment is complex and may arouse emotions and an ethos that is contrary to the culture of commerce. As multinational businesses expand their reach, they can be engines of wealth generation and peace. If on the other hand, global corporations adopt a martial ideology, then the hopes for human progress and cultural evolution will be dashed.

THE BUSINESS-WARRIOR MENTALITY

Throughout the evolution of marketing, as a result of increasing competition, there has been a shift from a production-oriented approach to a marketing-oriented approach. Strategic thinking that gives companies an advantage over their competitors has gained importance. By the end of the 1980s, experts studying strategy looked back into rich military literature to find some basic principles to help them define strategies for today's business environment. In this period, warfare and its similarities with the business world were a great inspiration for marketers. "The aim of this study is to show the relationship between marketing strategies and military strategies. This exploratory research used secondary data. It is expected that, in the twenty-first century's highly competitive conditions, this study will give marketers a different point of strategic view and contribute to marketing literature."

Three main periods can be observed in the evolution of marketing. These are the production-oriented period, the sales-oriented period, and the marketing-oriented period During the production-oriented period that prevailed until the 1930s, corporations were in the "I will sell whatever I produce" mindset because demand was higher than supply. Between 1930 and 1950, with the increased number of firms in the market, they had to focus on sales activities to get their products sold. A marketing-oriented approach was adopted after 1950, and there have been significant developments in strategic marketing since then. The number of studies on marketing strategies also increased in the 1980s, when competition became intense. This strategy is about creating a new market and making the competition irrelevant.

Art of War and Its Implications on Marketing Strategies

Developing military strategies goes back thousands of years. The oldest source on this subject is *The Art of War*, written by Chinese general and philosopher Sun Tzu on military strategies in the sixth century. The book was written with "the winning without fighting" approach and contains numerous aspects of war, including the planning stage, where internal and external conditions are analyzed, and sections on waging war, tactics, energy, opportunism, maneuvering, changing tactics, marching, terrain, nine kinds of battlegrounds, attack with fire, using spies and intelligence. *The 36 Secret Strategies of the Martial Arts* was inspired by Far Eastern martial arts and listed the methods that can be used in advantageous and disadvantageous situations. These strategies are mostly based on deluding the enemy. On the other hand, Prussian General Carl von Clausewitz's "On War" focuses on the unexpected, dynamic nature of military situations and emphasizes the importance of the flexibility principle in strategy.

Counterparts of Military Strategies in Marketing

While business professionals have long been using terms such as 'price wars,' 'market seizure,' and 'armament competition' for market competition, scholars saw marketing as a war in the early 1980s, researchers defined the market as "the battlefield where firms are fighting to seize consumers" and asserted that the need for businesses to develop competitor-oriented strategies to gain market share would push managers towards military science. Sun Tzu is the leading name in most studies on the relationship between marketing strategies and warfare. Many of the subjects that the Chinese philosopher considered in his book, *The Art of War*, can be adapted to the field of marketing. For instance, the stage of evaluating the conditions suggested by Sun Tzu is very similar to the SWOT analysis used by businesses in the strategic management process. Sun Tzu divides the environment into two categories: partially controllable factors and uncontrollable factors. The battlefield is a partially controllable factor, while weather conditions are an uncontrollable factor in the strategy literature, just as it is in economics and policy literature. Before deciding on their strategies, corporations should comprehensively analyze internal and external conditions and shape their strategies accordingly, as do parties at war. The counterparts of the concepts offered by Sun Tzu's work in marketing are below.

Sun Tzu: The Art of War Marketing
Laying a plan
Strategic planning
Waging a war
Marketing budget
Offensive Strategy
Marketing strategy
Tactics
Marketing tactics
Energy

Integrated marketing

Opportunism

Portfolio management

Maneuvering

Changing tactics

Marching

Aggressive marketing strategies

Terrain

Market field and market segmentation

The nine battlefields

Positioning

Attack by fire

Use of aggressive marketing tools

Use of spies

Use of marketing information systems

Equally as important as today's market structures, or today's technologies, or today's competitive advantage, is how the forces of change will affect a firm tomorrow and the day after.

But unfortunately, the instinctive habit of management is to look backward to the past to guide a course into the future. In an era characterized by a change conspiracy, this approach cannot succeed.

Military leaders are familiar with this problem. They call it "preparing to fight the last war." Such preparations, even fully implemented with rigor and discipline, consistently fail. Whether it's armored knights slaughtered by the crossbow, France's Maginot Line (a twentieth-century monument to backward thinking), the Polish horse cavalry that rode out to face Hitler's blitzkrieg, the American army reduced by Viet Cong guerrilla fighters, or civilian aircraft hijacked and turned into guided missiles, the history of warfare and of business is the history of innovations that render past strategies ineffective. Unfortunately, the misplaced focus is usually evident only in hindsight.

When wars, market share, jobs, or stock value have already been lost, for managers as for generals, hindsight is not sufficient. It is therefore essential to have an effective way not only to look toward the future but to create it. It is on this imperative that this report will concentrate.

INNOVATION

The term "creative destruction" gives us a warning, a name, and a general explanation for the waves of change that move continually through the marketplace, and it helps us direct our attention toward understanding the forces of change, rather than the illusion of stability. The term helps us see that the waves of change are themselves created, either intentionally or unintentionally, not by mysterious forces, but because of purposeful innovation in the competitive arena of the market.

However, innovation means different things to different people, and since it's a very important word to this report, we'll define it carefully.

We note, first of all, that the word "innovation" refers to an attribute, a process, and a result. Innovation happens somewhere in your company, or perhaps in someone's mind. The result, in any case, can be an insight, a new idea, a product, a strategy, or perhaps a new business process. It may be a question, a theory, or just a fear. But whatever it is, one quality that will distinguish the new thing is its "innovativeness."

This innovativeness refers to its distinctiveness, its originality, perhaps its usefulness, and most importantly its value.

"Innovation" also refers specifically to that new thing itself that the innovation process has produced. To be an innovation in business, the result must be increased value in the form of new or improved functionality, reduced cost, a price increase (good for the seller), a price decrease (good for the buyer), a better margin for the seller, or some combination thereof.

According to this definition, not every new or different idea qualifies as an innovation. Only a small percentage qualifies. Innovative ideas, by definition, create value for their users and valuable competitive advantage for their owners, and economic rewards. However, even innovations that do not have much impact on the market can be significant and critically important, especially if they help companies keep up with or surpass their competition.

In this context, innovation can defend, to block competitors from gaining our share even as it can also be used to attack. Hence, the approach that Peter Drucker labeled as "fastfollower" is a defensive strategy employed by companies to block the growing effectiveness of a competitor's offering. For example, Netscape Navigator had a strong head start in the browser market, but Microsoft's Internet Explorer quickly overtook Netscape and forced it to seek refuge as a subsidiary of AOL.

In high tech and particularly software markets, a variant on this strategy is known derisively as "vaporware." Here the defense consists of product announcements, not actual products. In the early days of the database market, vaporware announcements were prolific while actual new products came trotting along sometimes years later. In the course of one of these transitions, Borland died a quick death long before its promised software reached the market.

While these aspects of innovation and the innovation process occur in the life cycles of individual companies, innovation is also a significant factor in macroeconomics at the level of nations and the economy.

Economists know that it is only through effective innovation that real economic growth occurs because the underlying economic impact of innovation is to make resources more productive, which literally creates wealth for society. Hence, innovation is crucial to the economic viability of nations. But when discussing innovation, the focus must remain on individuals and individual companies, because their work drives the economy forward.

Just as innovators drive microeconomic change in specific markets and macroeconomic change in economies, innovators trigger creative destruction in their search for commercial success and competitive advantage.

Among the companies widely admired today most have attained their success precisely because they have innovated.

Through their innovations, they brought structural change to their markets; their motivation was to gain advantage within the capitalist process precisely as Schumpeter described.

But the innovator's role is only half of the equation. Customers are the ones who determine the real value of innovations because they are the ones who pay for them. Market behavior is an aggregate reflection of each consumer's drive to find the most attractive offers, and to maximize value received for cost incurred. As innovation is the process of creating higher value offerings, buyers naturally gravitate to innovative products.

But perhaps "gravitate" is the wrong word. Perhaps it is more accurate to say that capitalist markets devour innovations, hungrily consuming them the way a very hungry lion consumes a fresh kill. The capitalist system depends for its dynamism on the market's appetite for innovation, which has shown itself to be insatiable.

Inherent in the dynamics of market demand is the process that drives competition through innovation. The waves of change launched by innovators are countered by competitors who innovate to defend their existing positions or to attack with ambitions of their own.

This serves only to drive the process of change still that much faster throughout the economy. Accelerating change and the convergence in the marketplace of many competing innovators results in greater complexity for all, a landscape of acute danger and astonishing challenge. Any enterprise that intends to survive must somehow innovate because innovation itself is the only defense against innovation. Through innovation, you may catch up if you are behind, or even take the lead.

We see that the future of each and every firm is determined largely as a function of its ability to innovate effectively. Innovation is, therefore, a mandate, an absolute requirement for survival. And it is a problem.

A great, bumbling, stumbling problem, because managing the innovation process is one of the most challenging issues facing any organization. It is extraordinarily difficult to do well, in part because, as with top management, R&D organizations are often focused on the wrong objectives, as we will discuss below.

The Many Dimensions of Innovation

Creative destruction is fascinating from a macroeconomic perspective, and it raises tough microeconomic questions about change and change management in individual firms. It brings focus to how managers handle change, and it highlights the necessity of constant regeneration of the business from within through the R&D process and other creative endeavors.

While leaders of successful companies show a knack for reinventing their organizations in clever ways, among the failures we see repeatedly the consequences of not understanding or following Schumpeter's advice. Too many managers assume that change is the aberration, and they behave as if the market is stable. Perhaps the business school curriculum is partly at fault, for the very notion of a Master's in Business Administration assumes that the critical competence is administration, implying that continuing and well-controlled operation under managerial control is the focus, intent, and purpose of management.

For most managers, however, the ability to create is far more important than skills related to control. As Russ Ackoff points out, a serious flaw in the traditional MBA curriculum is that in the real world, managers are not presented with tidy and objective "cases" to solve - they must first figure out the problem, which can itself require a great deal of creativity. In reality, change is the norm and stability is an aberration.

Managers grapple with the disruptive forces of change, and they figure out for themselves what lessons and challenges are present in the current situation and what responses will be most effective in harnessing change so their organizations can survive.

In today's competitive environment, it's likely that somewhere a new innovation is about to appear that will dramatically affect current structures. Yet the relentless day to day demands on managers' time immerse them in a flood of pressing issues, and many simply fail to recognize important underlying factors that portend significant disruption. Managers tend not to account adequately for systemic change, and they are surprised and unprepared when they should not be.

Did personal computers and networked workstations surprise the computer industry? Absolutely.

Did the high-performance sports shoe surprise the staid sneaker marketplace when Nike invented the category?

Did efficient and high-quality Japanese cars surprise the Detroit automakers? Did the cellular telephone shock the entrenched Telco's? Yes, yes, and yes. Occasionally, we even see a company whose leaders, judging by the evidence of their behavior, prefer to close rather than do the work of adapting to change.

RCA, Woolworth's, Smith-Corona, and Polaroid are recent examples.

As it is imperative for the organization to be continually engaged in the process of innovation, the question is where efforts to innovate should be focused. There are, it turns out, many possibilities. To examine these possibilities, we devised an imaginary and archetypal large organization with products and services in many markets, extensive operations in numerous locations, and a predominantly internal support structure. We find that in such an organization, there are at least thirty-seven distinctive opportunities for innovation.

- Business structure
- Alliances
- Capital formation
- Administration
- Information flow
- Automation
- In sourcing/outsourcing services
- Organization
- Structure type
- Facilities infrastructure
- IT infrastructure
- Employee/contractor mix
- Employee experience
- Decision-making processes
- Facilities effectiveness
- Process to improve processes
- Customer experience
- Communication process
- Brand/image
- Advertising
- Feedback

- Customer service
- Service process
- Communication
- Supply chain
- Distribution system
- Manufacturing
- Communication
- Product
- Product offering
- Product availability
- Technology (hidden)
- Technology (evident)
- Manufacturing
- R&D
- User interface
- Packaging
- Functionality
- Life cycle model
- Sales model
- Sustainability
- After-sale service
- Distribution

The first thing that jumps out from this list is that the clear majority of these opportunities do not involve new technologies embedded in existing or new products. Despite the widely-held assumption to the contrary, "innovation" is by no means limited to "technology." The lesson: technology innovation by itself has rarely been sufficient to ensure the future, and it is certainly not today. Interestingly, this is the case even when innovative technology is at the core of the offering. A good example is Xerox. Chester Carlson's technological innovation was a stunning breakthrough and a testimony to his insight and persistence.

The Xerox story is also testimony to the difficulties of fore-casting the market for genuinely new products. Many industrial giants of the day, including IBM, Kodak, and GE, each rejected Carlson's technology.

When he finally found a partner, tiny Haloid Company, getting the technology to market entailed far more than simply building new machines. The success of the company in its early years was due to its innovative approach to distribution leasing the machines on a per-use basis instead of selling them outright.

Today, however, Xerox is a company in difficulty, threatened by far more creative competitors whose own innovations in distribution and technology have surpassed Xerox's. Again and again, we see the inexorability of creative destruction.

Did Xerox top management believe that the market was stable and that their incumbent competitive advantages would persist? If so, they were clearly mistaken, and now another generation of top management has the task of cleaning up a mess.

But the problem was not that Xerox did not recognize the importance of innovation. They generously funded technical R&D that surpassed the efforts of most other companies, creating the legendary Palo Alto Research Center, PARC, from which sprang an amazing string of enormous breakthroughs in many dimensions of technology.

Even as the company entered its period of decline, it was still producing astonishing technological breakthroughs. Its Docutech system, for example, a self-contained digital printing plant and bindery, did what no copier had done before. But within a relatively short while, Xerox competitors had machines that matched or surpassed the Docutech in every respect.

This illustrates one of the most vexing problems associated with technological innovation: in today's environment, technology is one thing that a determined and adequately-financed competitor may readily replicate or bypass. Patents offer limited protection, but sometimes they simply provide stimulus and insight for others determined to be still more inventive.

For this reason, investor Warren Buffet has said that he does not invest in technology companies. He has recognized that the underlying rate of change in technology markets is so fast it simply does not allow sufficient defensible competitive advantage.

A focus on technology breakthroughs to the exclusion of other aspects of innovation is misplaced. Given the complexity inherent in today's technologies, you simply can't count on being able to out-R&D the market on a consistent enough basis to sustain a competitive advantage. Sooner or later, and probably sooner, every technology meets its match or its superior, and it's probably coming from a competitor.

But for the brief interval while a particular technology is superior, it can be the basis upon which to build something of truly critical importance: strong relationships with customers. Innovation efforts must therefore include the creation of new approaches that help strengthen the bonds with customers, and they should draw from any of the thirty-seven dimensions that might provide differentiation. Strong customer relationships help companies survive the inevitable periods when their technology will not be the best. The experience of another technology giant, IBM, underscores the significance of innovation that is not just technological.

Over the years, many of ibm's successes have come not as a result of technological leadership, but because of its close relationships with its customers. IBM is not actually a technology leader in many of its product areas, but for decades, IT managers have struggled with the choice between leading edge technology offered by IBM's competitors, and IBM's own systems which were often just slightly above average.

But even though its technology may not have been the best, IBM made sure that it was a safe choice for customers because the company made consistent and unsurpassed efforts to provide exemplary service. The adage was that nobody ever got fired for choosing IBM. Now we see that over the years an increasing proportion of IBM's revenues and profits have come from its services organization. By 2002, services accounted for more than 50% of revenues. So is IBM a computer company? Well, yes. Its high-profile research efforts in areas such as super high-density magnetic storage drives and the Deep Blue chess-playing supercomputer are well-publicized initiatives that keep this idea in the public's mind.

But the IBM services organization is far more significant today because the relationships created and sustained through services are the real key to the company's future. Ford provides another clear example. The original Ford cars of the early 1900s were innovative for automotive engineering but equally important to the company's success was the innovative production process (the first vertically integrated assembly line), the distribution system (the dealer network), and the company's pricing model that ensured affordability.

These innovations enabled Ford to create an enduring relationship with American car-buyers and build a significant share of the market. By the 1920s, however, GM had copied and caught up with Ford's innovations and introduced some of its own. A minor GM innovation with major impact was the availability of cars in colors other than black. Ford suffered steady decline thereafter and was rescued from what might have been fatal demise only by the enormous demand for military vehicles caused by World War II. After the war, the company soon staggered again and was nearly bankrupt by the late 1950s.

The Ford story illustrates two important aspects of competition in nearly every market. First, each industry has its own rhythm of technical innovation, driven largely by advances in materials and methods. These advances often lead to cycles of changing market dominance. In the auto industry, Ford was supplanted by GM, and more recently GM by Toyota and Honda.

The second aspect, however, is what seriously complicates the focus on technology. Ford's choice of black paint was an economic one, part of a relentless strategy of minimizing costs. From 1903 through World War I, this strategy was a significant contributor to the company's success. But in the 20s, the nature of the market itself was changing, and Ford's success as a cost cutting pioneer did not serve him when market dynamics began to favor factors related to comfort and style.

Within the framework of any market cycle, a company can grasp and sustain leadership, but the greater challenge is managing what happens when a new cycle begins. Very few companies sustain leadership positions beyond a single cycle because they don't grasp the significance of change. Too often they rely on technology to provide differentiation, and technologies are so frequently surpassed. While one set of products and services may be exceptionally well-suited to the market at a particular point in time, it's rare for a company to adapt its products and services to changing market conditions quickly enough to sustain the leadership position.

Companies, therefore, cede market dominance when their competitors attack them in areas where they are not prepared to defend themselves. Chances are, they have positioned their defenses so it leaves them vulnerable. Sears, for example, allowed Wal-Mart to establish itself in the smaller rural markets that Sears had abandoned or ignored. Wal-Mart then applied innovation processes throughout its growing supply chain to lower its overall operating costs, at which point it went after Sears and Kmart in their urban markets. Sears became a second-tier player almost before it realized what had happened, while K-Mart eventually found itself in bankruptcy.

Similarly, by focusing on annual style changes in their competition with one another, the Detroit automakers overlooked the importance of underlying quality improvements. When quality suddenly became an important attribute for American buyers, the Japanese manufacturers took market share. Before 1980, GM didn't take the Japanese seriously as competitors, and it didn't take quality seriously either. Today GM is still struggling to catch up to Japanese quality standards, and as a result, GM's share of the American car market declined from 50% to less than 35% between 1980 and 2000. It takes exceptional discipline and clarity of vision to defend a competitive advantage and carry it through to a next generation of offerings. With success comes growth, and as a company increases in size and scope, the nature of management's challenges change considerably. Managing Xerox at the start-up stage was an entirely different problem than steering the global copier colossus.

When a company is small, top management is usually in direct contact with customers as a natural part of its role in the company. But as managers deal with the complexities of larger enterprises and multiplying layers of organization, they become further and further removed from a direct experience of the market. Without direct contact, they are intuitively forced to rely on past experiences, and they have a progressively more difficult time hearing the voice of the market.

In addition, the need for extensive administration ultimately distracts management from the business of innovation, while dysfunctional and bureaucratic behaviors grow endemic inside of large organizations and result in huge distortions to the flow of information. Corporate politics gets more attention, and emphasis shifts to internal events, while key external factors become obscured from view. Meanwhile, change waits for no organization, and innovations from competitors are introduced without sufficient response. In the 1950s, IBM's mainframe business, though dominant, was a tiny thing compared to its size a decade later. It's one thing to be an innovator in a small market, and quite a different matter to bring creative drive to a large operation.

As a company grows and the stakes become higher, the risks

that the small company has taken as a matter of course are now subjected to a lot more scrutiny, and reaction times slow. More levels of management have a stake in major decisions; time lags in decision making are longer. In extreme cases, "analysis paralysis" sets in.

Smaller, more nimble competitors have less to lose, fewer people to convince, and often a sense of desperation that sharpens top management's perception of market needs. The well-tuned senses of entrepreneurial top managers become magnets for capital – small new companies are founded specifically to attack new market niches that only their top managers even recognize.

The result is a pattern that repeats with astonishing regularity. As innovative companies grow they become followers rather than leaders. But their sheer size, combined with control of distribution channels, makes them formidable competitors even when their later innovations are really copies.

Another factor heavily influencing market evolution is that at any given time in any given market, only a few critical value dimensions yield the key combination that proves most attractive to customers.

Whichever company has just the right mix gains a temporary advantage, but the emphasis remains on "temporary" because the market's need change and very few companies sustain leadership over a long period.

We find countless examples of companies that have distinguished themselves by focusing on one or another of the many dimensions of innovation but then fade into obscurity when the dimension in which they were particularly strong became a secondary or tertiary concern of customers. From a manager's perspective, thirty-seven dimensions of innovation present a daunting challenge. Even if you're GE, GM, or IBM, thirty-seven arenas for innovation are clearly too many to address at once. This brings us to a critical dilemma that confronts managers every day:

how to choose. In what aspects of a business should efforts at innovation be focused?

Should a company apply itself to innovation in its products and services, or its brand, or its organization, its leadership team, its technology, its capital structure, or any of the others among the possible targets? Or should it choose any of them?

Individual factors may explain the success achieved by this or that company in this or that market, but while any of the thirty-seven areas may be important, no one of them consistently explains emerging success and failure. Wouldn't it be far more useful to have a robust explanation of the emergent successes and the astonishing failures, and thereby a better way to both examine the competition and direct innovation efforts?

COMPETITION & BUSINESS MODELS

W hen you look at our list of thirty-seven possible innovation targets you see interesting potentials, but you also see a fragmented world. Viewed as a list of possibilities, each target stands separately, interesting perhaps, but alone. This may be useful for analytical purposes, but it's also fundamentally distorted because by looking at inventory parts you'll surely not get a real appreciation for the whole.

But what if you could look at the problem of innovation as one process? What would you see?

You might see this: yesterday a whole range of tough competitors were creating new products, services, distribution systems, brands, and infrastructures bringing change to the market today. Recognizing the imminence of the creative destruction that will result from this, we accept the absolute imperative of innovation. And now we are confronted with this question: How do we innovate with a clear focus not on the parts of the system, but the system as a whole?

To accomplish this, we would first have to understand what the "whole system" is. It's not a particular department, a product, a service, or a brand. It is the entire organization together as one thing, working together to deliver value. For this new integrated whole to be a useful managerial concept, we must give it a name and design a process through which it can help us manage the enterprise more effectively.

This whole is the "business model," a comprehensive description of business as an integrated system functioning in an intimate relationship with the broader market. In this concept, the individual components of an organization do not matter as much as the way they work together to enable the organization to create value and deliver it to customers.

A business model is, therefore, a description of a whole system, a combination of products and services delivered to the market in a particular way, or ways, supported by an organization, positioned according to a particular branding that, most importantly, yields a particular set of strong relationships with present and future customers. Further, a business model describes how the experiences of creating and delivering value may evolve along with the changing needs and preferences of customers.

Understanding Systems and Business Models

To make this approach useful, we first need to understand some critical characteristics of the whole. We need to know how this whole differs from the parts that comprise it.

A key insight is that the distinguishing characteristic of any system is that its outputs emerge not because of any single part but because of the way the parts are connected together. An excellent example of connectedness is an airplane. Each of an airplane's components and even its major sub-assemblies have the absolute tendency to fall towards the ground. Take them up to 35,000 feet and let go, and they invariably tumble straight down. It is only when all the parts are assembled just so, and working together properly, that the system we call the airplane manifests "air paleness" and actually flies.

Similarly, a system we call "a company" consists of many parts. It participates in other systems we call "markets," which are part of a still larger system we call "the economy." If you take a part of a company - say the accounting department – and put it into a market by itself, what you have is approximately... nothing. The accounting department has no relevance outside of the larger company because accounting is only meaningful when transactions have to be accounted for.

Similarly, manufacturing requires a sales force, distribution, and customers. Marketing has no purpose independent of a company's identity, its products and services, and the perceptions of outsiders. This tells us that the success of a company is not attributable just to one or another part, just as the reality of flight is not an attribute of a single part of the airplane.

There's another aspect of the airplane analogy that's also important, one that has to do with the process of optimization. Let's say we have a nicely functioning airplane and we want to improve it. We might want to make the engines more powerful so the plane can go faster.

But that might put too much stress on the airframe or the wings, or it might change the control properties of the plane and make it impossible to fly. Hence, the ability of the system to function depends entirely on the mutual fitness of the parts. No part can possibly be optimized except in the context of all the rest. Instead, we must direct our efforts toward optimizing the system as a whole.

The product that cannot reach the customer provides no value; the service that cannot be delivered provides no value; distribution systems lacking effective products provide no value. So the optimal approach to marketing depends on the actual products that you're manufacturing and the customers for whom they're intended. Manufacturing, marketing, and sales must fit together, and the definition of this fitness is the business model.

Consider a few somewhat oversimplified examples of what happens when the parts don't fit together well. Imagine a company with an amazing breakthrough technology, but a sales force incapable of selling it and a senior management largely indifferent to prospective buyers. Actually, that's not so difficult to imagine, nor is it all that oversimplified. Xerox had this experience.

Xerox is the company that for all intents and purposes invented the personal computer at PARC back in the early 1970s. Naturally, Xerox wanted to make money from this profound invention, but because Xerox management didn't actually understand who would use the product, or what for, they tried to push it through an entirely unsuited distribution channel, to a market that was neither prepared for it nor able to understand it. It went nowhere.

Well, it went nowhere for Xerox. But a few other companies made excellent use of Xerox technology and in later years they have made billions - yes, billions - by applying Xerox inventions to their own products and services. Apple, Microsoft, and 3COM were three big beneficiaries, and none have paid so much as a dime in royalties to Xerox.

Now imagine a company with a brilliant sales force also adept at bringing back news from the marketplace, but the company ignores the warnings. This happened to IBM when it overlooked the emerging workstation market and allowed Sun to become the market leader when IBM failed to even make an attempt to address the new client-server IT paradigm. Or let's look at cars. Gm's vast dealer network is deeply embedded in the commercial fabric throughout North America (and, in fact, the entire world), but the company somehow can't produce an Oldsmobile-branded car that enough people actually want to buy. The pipeline is there, but little is coming through it, so GM has been compelled by its persistent lack of innovation to shut down the Oldsmobile line.

To repeat, then, a "business model" is a description of the entire marketplace and the relationship of the company to that commercial environment. It is a precise definition of who customers are and how the company intends to satisfy their needs both today and tomorrow.

A business model also includes a specific assessment of today's competitors, and tomorrow's, and the technologies that will be embedded in various competing versions of products and services. Had Xerox been thinking about its personal computer technology in terms of a business model, perhaps the results would have been different. Had IBM understood that workstation computing was a new and important business model, perhaps Sun would never have attained prominence. Had GM considered the business model underlying its Oldsmobile line, perhaps it would still be viable. In each example, it is impossible to know the root causes of the problem without knowing the actual people involved, but the results strongly suggest that top management was probably not asking the right questions, and they were probably not having the right conversations about the future and how to adapt to it.

The realization that for the company it is the business model that matters drives a new approach the competitive marketplace and the way that companies should organize themselves to compete. It gives us a new way to think about adapting to change, or how to create it. Today and going forward what we're talking about is not just competition between companies, but competition between business models. In other words, Business Model Warfare.

Business model warfare characterizes winning and losing that marks the creatively destructive marketplace, enables us to define a set of principles and skills that will enable managers to be effective at this game. Not that it's a new game; this is the way business has always been, and for just as long managers have been falling into the trap of focusing too much on today and not enough on tomorrow.

Winning and Losing at Business Model Warfare

As we have noted, in addition to erroneous assumptions about stability, managers also fall into the trap of focusing too much of their attention inside their own organizations. This is a particular danger with middle managers under pressure from the hierarchy of organizational authority. Their instinctive sense of self-preservation forces them to pay great attention to the behavior of senior management and often less attention to customers.

To engage in business model warfare, managers cannot be internally focused on products, services, or administration to excluding the critical relationships between these elements and the even more crucial interactions between a company and its customers. Thinking about innovation in the business model as a matter of the overall relationship between the company and its customers, rather than innovation isolated in this or that aspect, may, therefore, yield greater insight and better management performance.

It's not a coincidence that the winners in business model warfare are usually those who manage their customer relationships effectively. Here are some examples.

Japanese auto manufacturers are the source of many business model innovations. They applied their increasing expertise in manufacturing quality to create new, affordable, high-end product lines, and now Lexus, Acura, and Infiniti are among the most admired cars worldwide and the most profitable segments of their businesses. They continue to steadily increase their share of the American auto market, and their innovations in alternative fuels, far before American manufacturers, may also win them added market share in the future, as buyers develop a preference for fuels other than oil.

European giants Auchan and Carrefour redefined the French grocery business in the 1960s by applying new cash register technology to create the hypermarket, and at about the same time, Novotel introduced a new kind of hotel.

In the 1970s, Nike redefined competition in the sports shoe and sports apparel business by transforming star athletes into marketing icons, first with runner Steve Prefontaine, and later with Michael Jordan. In so doing, Nike created new markets for its shoes and clothing and surpassed Adidas to become the global leader in a ruptured market.

Nike's core business model innovation was turning its brand into a key element in the self-identification of its customers, which comes close to the ideal when we're talking about the company-customer relationship.

American Express once dominated the credit card industry and carefully cultivated an image of prestige and exclusivity. Visa entered into competition by creating a global network far more fluid and flexible and has now surpassed American Express. Visa charged lower rates to merchants, making its services more attractive, and built its brand on ubiquity - Visa cards are available everywhere. While each individual issuer has its own cards, the Visa brand cleverly maintains its underlying presence, since it is owned by its member banks—all 65,65,000. This is an organizational innovation of the first caliber, developed by Dee Hock and now articulated by him as an example of the "chaordic" organization, one that effectively balances chaos and order in service to continuous adaptation.

Dell created a commercial powerhouse by completely reinventing the manufacturing and distribution process and building machines to order, rather than to inventory, introducing an entirely new business model to the personal computer industry. Mass customization at a competitive price defined a new kind of customer relationship in the PC industry. Southwest Airlines developed an approach to the airline business unlike the airlines established when the company was founded and has sustained its unique business model to become the most financially successful company in a highly-troubled industry.

One of the most interesting things about Southwest is there isn't much technology evident in the business. What is apparent is that the leaders of Southwest thought through the air travel business in a comprehensive way and avoided falling into traps that have hurt others. The company is not burdened by restrictive labor agreements that now weigh so heavily on its competitors, by design, the company does not operate out of airports that charge high fees, and it does not participate in centralized reservations systems.

The company has not attempted to be something that it is not, a mighty global airline, but has instead focused on understanding its niche and serving it profitably. Today the market value of Southwest is more than twice that of United, American, and Delta Airlines combined. Yet the revenues of Southwest are a small fraction of any of them. Why is this? Because Southwest is the only airline that's profitable.

The company has a business model entirely suited to its market, and investors reasonably believe that it has the best prospects in the industry. Tomorrow, it's possible that a competitor's innovation or some other change in the market landscape could change that perception, but for today the market has expressed its expectations.

UNDERSTANDING CUSTOMERS

As we examine industry after industry, we see that wherever there is an exemplar, a company that stands head and shoulders above others, that company is almost always a business model innovator that is applying creativity in dimensions other than technology to become a market leader. This does not, however, mean that every business model innovator is also a market leader, for innovation is a risky enterprise. Many new business models fail, as we have seen with the collapse of the short-lived internet boom.

Like Southwest, FedEx is most notable not simply for the pioneering idea of overnight delivery, nor for its innovative use of information technology to track packages, nor is it positioning itself as a reliable, courteous, and service-oriented alternative to the post office. It is all of these factors, and more, integrated together as a coherent system. The fusion of these elements into an effective organization is precisely what we mean by the business model, and when we compare the FedEx model with the US Post Office model, we see consistent innovation on one side and astonishing stagnation on the other.

FedEx has a history of change and development that the post office lacks. Certainly, the post office is hampered by its own history as a government agency, its rigid labor relations, and even by its extremely broad mission. Just as certainly, we see a business model failing, one losing market share to a host of competitors and becoming marginalized on the fringe of economic viability.

It's interesting to see how the post office attempted to defend itself from FedEx. In the mid-1990s, the post office introduced a guaranteed two-day delivery service in a package very similar to FedEx's, available at just 25% of the cost. After a while, however, it became apparent that two-day service wasn't actually a guarantee, just an intention. While for many customers this may have been acceptable, it shows how little the post office management understood that FedEx's reputation for reliable execution was as important as the idea of its timely deliveries. Aside from the questionable notion of what constitutes acceptable delivery, it's probably a moot point until the post office realizes that another element of its business model is obsolete, namely the requirement that customers must wait in long lines to get service.

If the post office ever wises up and solves either or both problems, FedEx will have someone besides the brown trucks of UPS to worry about. In contrast, UPS has carefully followed innovations from FedEx with its own, and now with its acquisition of Mail Boxes Etc. it has introduced a new dimension to competition among package delivery services.

How will FedEx respond to this new maneuver in the business model war?

Home depot also exemplifies the successful integration of numerous factors to create a business that is appealing to customers and so devastating to competitors. The impressive scale on two dimensions gigantic stores and a huge number of them leads to high sales volume that enables the company to charge the lowest prices. The local hardware store or lumber yard can't compete unless it, too, undertakes its own business model innovation and positions itself as something that Home Depot cannot be. Which would be highly personalized service, fast transactions, proximity, better selection, different products ....

What we see consistently across these examples, and with widespread consistency across the entire history of business, is that it's rarely, if ever, a single innovation that propels a business to success. It is, instead, a suite of innovations that complement one another and work together to provide a novel or distinctive value proposition that underlies success. The key is not necessarily the product or service itself - which could be highly innovative or even just acceptable - but something brought to market in an innovative way, supported in an innovative way, branded in an innovative way, but in the end always an approach that builds enduring relationships between the company and its customers.

The core of the innovation value proposition need not be built around a technology, per se. In the examples cited above - Toyota, Honda, Nissan, Nike, Visa, Dell, FedEx, Home Depot, Southwest Airlines, and Ford (in the early days) - proprietary technologies play a part in the company's success, but there is always much more. The key to success is a focus not on technology itself, but technology applied in a business process to optimize the relationship between the company and its customers. In today's environment, nearly any technology can be, has been, and will be copied, so the important competitive advantage is knowing how to use technology so it adds the greatest value for customers.

It's when enough people believe that a $50,000 Nissan performs as well as or better than a $65,000 Mercedes that the structure of the market undergoes a profound change. With this in mind, we now have a better way to characterize marketplace competition, creative destruction, and innovation. We see that effective innovation is not a matter of exploiting individual technologies nor of exceptional performance in any other individual element of a business, but rather a matter of harnessing the business model itself, which may but does not necessarily include technologies among its many possible dimensions.

To state it more simply, what's happening continuously in the marketplace is competition between business models themselves. The Lexus business model differs from Ford's business model or Daimler Chrysler's, etc.

What this means is the winners at business model warfare have generally applied innovation to create competitive advantages, building stronger relationships with customers by developing business models that fit closely with customer needs and preferences. Winners who have figured out these principles then seek to sustain their advantages through further business model innovations that defend newly-won territory and extend into new domains. It is, therefore, the business model itself that must be the focus of innovation, and innovation in any or all of the thirty-seven possible dimensions must be undertaken in service to a larger framework that is defined by the business model itself.

SUMMARY OF BUSINESS MODEL WARFARE

We will summarize our concept of business model warfare in three propositions:

One: A "business model" defines a broad competitive approach to business and articulates how a company applies processes and technologies to build and sustain effective relationships with customers. These relationships are the most critical factor. Creating them, understanding them, preserving them, enriching them, and extending them are the critical attributes of success. Everything that is done must be in service to these relationships; they are the point.

Two: Every successful business model earns some sort of competitive advantage to the extent that it serves successful relationships. However, any advantage may disappear overnight should a competitor devise a superior model, thereby displacing the company in the relationship with the customer. The lifespan of any business model is therefore limited, and due to the general unpredictability of change, its timeframe is indeterminate. Managers with the good fortune to preside over a successful business model should never lose sight of the ephemeral nature of their advantages and must focus not on administering the (illusory) stability of today, but on preparing for or precipitating the inevitable change of tomorrow.

Three: Since business models are a more comprehensive way of understanding the focus of competition, they must also be the focus of innovation. Relentlessly changing conditions means that business models evolve rapidly, and business model innovation is therefore not optional. While innovations in any area within an organization may be important, innovations that pertain broadly and directly to the business model will be life-sustaining. Based on what we have discussed here, the pattern of company mortality is a real and significant phenomenon, a result of the acceleration of change throughout the economy that operates on both demand and supply.

Demand is enormously influenced by innovation - new products and services coming into the market affect the fate of all market participants.

The perspective from the supply side is more complicated, but the pattern is also evident. Because the market is so transparent and the performance of every public company is subject to detailed scrutiny by investors and analysts, subtle changes in an organization's performance can lead to broad swings in stock price.

Improving performance and increasing stock price are a self-feeding cycles that create more favorable conditions for companies to develop and implement future innovations, both by improving stock currency for making acquisitions and by lowering the overall cost of capital. Conversely, declining performance and a falling stock price can lead to a downward spiral that makes it progressively more difficult for companies to compete for attractive acquisition fodder, and which can also increase the cost of capital that could be invested in innovation-related activities such as R&D and product development. Get ahead and push farther ahead; get behind and fall farther behind.

The data cited here show that over the medium term the majority of companies will get trapped in the downward spiral and one way or another most will disappear.

The prevalence of this trap suggests that while managers may be thinking and worrying about change and its impact on their companies, about competition, and about competitive advantage, they must be doing so in a way that is simply not effective. Hence, we suggest that thinking about and enacting business model innovation may be a productive remedy for established businesses.

But the need for good thinking about business models is as important for new businesses as it is for old ones, and among the many examples considers the spectacular rise and equally spectacular collapse of Web van, in which more than a billion dollars of capital was invested and lost. Its management - including a renowned CEO who had formerly been the head of Andersen Consulting - was so confident of what they were doing that they invested hundreds of millions of dollars of capital in a distribution infrastructure, even though market demand that would generate a return was unproven.

They believed that they could make the business work, and apparently fooled themselves into thinking that their own belief was sufficient basis for betting their capital on a business model that had never actually been fully tested. In the end, hundred-million-dollar warehouses were built but never used, never generating even a cent of return.

In spite of abundant talk about change, the temptation to build a business according to a fixed structure expected to endure for the long term remains strong. Never mind that the long-term is completely unpredictable. Another way to say this is that management remains unrepentantly focused on stability and continuity, instead of on disruption and change.

It remains relevant to discuss managing for change as an absolute requirement, but many managers still aren't very good at dealing with it. Nevertheless, recognizing change in the marketplace and adapting to its turbulent evolution are the realities that confront all executives, for although we remember periods that seemed stable, they are in fact long gone and never to return.

As markets continue to evolve and competition becomes ever more demanding, engaging in Business Model Warfare, therefore, becomes not just an interesting possibility, but perhaps a requirement. To survive, all organizations must develop a comprehensive innovation framework, and the perspective offered by the Business Model Warfare framework can help leaders to be more effective.

When we look at the business world, it's clear that the story of change is still the important story to tell and leading an organization in the face of change remains the critical skill.

CONCLUSIONS

Generally, on a market disputed by two giants, there should not be any opportunity for a newcomer except with immense financial efforts. That a small operator became a medium-large operator in such a small period proves the low reaction power of the leaders. The Company could have used these facts alone to raise its notoriety among the customers, seeding a feeling of doubt regarding its competitors.

Second, there are facts that indicate that the usage of military strategies and principles aided in the process of entering the market. The decisive way all the actions were performed, the concentration of all the available resources to achieve the goal, the way the least disputed market sectors were identified and used and that priorities were established based on the actions of the competitors, were undeniably effective to fulfill the main objectives of the Company.

SIMILARITIES BETWEEN SUN TZU AND DAVIDSON'S IDEAS

Marketing studies that refer to military literature use various classifications for military strategies. In *The Art of War*, the basic war strategies are defense, offense, flanking offense, and guerrilla (Garsombke, 1987). In marketing warfare, defensive strategy is appropriate for the leader, while offense is for challengers. Flank strategy is for firms aiming at certain market segments, and guerrilla strategy is good for small firms (Tino, 1987). Meanwhile, in their article titled "Marketing Warfare in the 1980s," Kotler and Singh (1981) looked at marketing warfare strategies in two groups: defensive and offensive strategies. In an article published anonymously on the internet, the most effective military strategies in history are said to be the crescent strategy, shock and awe, blitzkrieg, and guerrilla warfare, all of which can be considered offensive strategies. The rest of this study will be based on the defensive and offensive strategies from the military literature that Kotler and Singh (1981) adapted to marketing, and other strategies in the book will be included under these categories.

Researchers asserted that defensive strategies should be used by market leaders that wish to prevent strong maneuvers by their competitors. These protect the market share of the corporation, to sustain its profitability and positioning (Bogdan et al., 2008). According to this view, the market leader that adopts defensive strategies will defend itself against competitors and strengthen its own position by preventing new threats (new products, new promotional activities and additional services), while it forces its competitor to exhaust its valuable resources (Garsombke, 1987).

The six defensive strategies that have been adapted to marketing from military literature are position defense, mobile defense, preemptive defense, flank positioning defense, counteroffensive defense, and strategic withdrawal. The defensive strategies are summarized below (Kotler and Singh, 1981; Tek,1999; Kotler and Keller, 2009).

Position Defense: The conventional concept of defense is closely related to the reinforcement of the fort. Almost all forts in history have failed in war situations. This strategy is one of the riskiest military strategies. The best counterpart to this concept in the business world is marketing myopia. According to this view, the biggest mistake that a powerful brand can make is to believe that growth and profitability will continue. The biggest mistake that a market leader under attack can make is to use all its resources to reinforce the fort around its existing products. According to this view, the best approach for firms that want to avoid this mistake is to reduce risk by expanding towards similar or different fields.

Mobile Defense: Mobile defense is expansion towards new fields that the firm can use for defense or counter-offensives in the future. This expansion is done through market expansion and diversification, rather than by increasing the number of brands.

Pre-emptive Defense: Pre-emptive defense is based on the principle that prevention is more advantageous than fighting, and it includes many offensive strategies. For instance, a firm can block a competitor whose market share is rising by finding its weaknesses or by encircling it. Another example of this strategy is market leaders blocking their competitors with new technologies.

Flank Positioning Defense: Flank positioning defense is creating a blockade that will stop the enemy. In this strategy, potential threats should be carefully analyzed, and flanks should be reinforced accordingly. It is easy to find examples of firms (e.g. Coca-Cola) that use flank positioning defense in the business world. The firm launched Diet Coke before Pepsi Cola and gained power in this segment before its competitor could. The leader of the razor blade market, Gillette, entered the female products market and got an edge over competitors that entered the market later.

Counteroffensive Defense: This is the counteroffensive reaction of the party in the defensive position. For instance, when Oxy5 reinforced its acne medication with powerful promotional activities, Clearasil responded by increasing its promotional activities. Sometimes when the market share is being lost too fast, it is obligatory to respond with counteroffensives. When Gillette gained power in the Turkish market, Derby responded counter-offensively with an intense marketing campaign using its newly created Ali Desidero character.

Strategic Withdrawal: Strategic withdrawal, which is considered neither offense nor defense by certain sources, is a maneuver where a firm can focus on important points to secure its market power and to be able launch counteroffensives. For instance, Westinghouse used the strategic withdrawal strategy by reducing the number of its refrigerator models from forty to thirty.

OFFENSIVE STRATEGIES

Offensive strategies are used by challenger firms to increase their market share (Bogdan et al., 2008). These are usually recommended for second and third-ranking firms in the market. In this strategy, the challenger firm finds the Achilles heel of the leader and attacks this point with full force. This offensive strategy is based on finding the weakness of the leader, rather than a head-on collision. The leader's weakness can be in a range of fields from product features to consumer service. The challenger can improve its product with new features or try to offer better customer service (Garsombke, 1987). Offensive strategy types are a frontal attack, flanking attack, encirclement, bypass attack and guerrilla warfare. The offensive strategies are summarized below (Kotler and Singh, 1981; Tek,1999; Kotler and Keller, 2009).

Frontal Attack: In a frontal attack the challenger attacks the leader's front lines with full force. The aim is not the weak side, but the strong side of the competitor. In order for this strategy to be successful, the offensive party must have an absolute advantage over its competitor. According to military doctrine, possessing three times more power than the competitor is necessary for successful frontal attack. For instance, GE and Xerox overlooked IBM's powerful defense and failed in their frontal attack. Firms that use this strategy mostly do so with low pricing. Another method is to invest in R&D to lower production costs.

Flanking Attack: The strongest point of an army on the battlefield is the point where it will attack or where it expects to be attacked. Flanks and sides are naturally weak, therefore they are the best places to attack. In modern offensive warfare, the main principle is to focus power on the weak side. This strategy is especially appropriate for firms with more limited resources than their competitor. Flanking attacks can be applied on two strategic dimensions. The first is to attack geographical areas where the competitor is absent, and the second is to attack market segments that the competitor is not providing for. Flanking attacks are one of the strongest traditions of modern marketing philosophy and have a higher chance of success than frontal attacks.

Encirclement: In flanking attacks, places where the competitor is absent are targeted, while in encirclement the competitor is approached from multiple directions. The aim is to attack the competitor from multiple points to make it defend itself on all sides. An example of this strategy is Seiko's attack from every direction by producing various models. If the competitor does not leave any points to attack, or these points are not created, flanking attack turns out to be a frontal attack and three times more power than the competitor is required. (Bozkurt & Ergen/International Journal of Research in Business and Social Science)

Bypass Attack: Bypass attack is most indirect attack at the competitor, and it is similar to cold war during peace. Here we are talking about skipping the enemy, attacking easier territories and developing these areas. This kind of attack in marketing can manifest itself as diversification in unrelated products or entering new markets with existing products. This strategy was used successfully in 1971, when Colgate abandoned its domestic market, entered new markets, and added new products to its line to compete with Proctor & Gamble.

Guerrilla Warfare: Guerrilla warfare is a good strategy for firms that are challenging but have limited resources. In this strategy small, intermittent attacks are organized against different aspects of the enemy to disturb and demoralize the competitor. Traditional and nontraditional guerrilla warfare methods are used to disturb and wear out the competitor. The first person to bring this up in marketing was Jay Conrad Levinson. Levinson (1985) asserted that a firm should focus its energy and resources on customers rather than competition and described various methods for small and medium firms to influence potential customers. This strategy manifests itself in the business world as selective price reductions, intervening in suppliers, pressuring the management, intense promotional attacks, and legal action towards the competitor. The strength of guerrilla warfare stems from these factors:

The guerrilla preserves its resources since the competitor is never confronted.

Guerrilla power is very flexible and can be adapted to both offensive and defensive operations.

It is difficult to respond to guerrilla warfare with classical methods.

Guerrilla strategies are suitable for small firms with high flexibility and limited resources. A small firm can easily withdraw from the market or change its product line and management objectives.

The Most Effective Military Strategies in History

The four most effective military strategies in history, according to internet sources, are crescent, shock and awe, blitzkrieg, and guerrilla warfare, all of which are found scattered in academic sources. They are also all offensive. guerrilla warfare is found in many sources on military strategy, while the other three are not found in main sources. But they are also described below, as they are complementary to guerrilla warfare.

Crescent Strategy: The fundamental strategy, especially in Eastern societies, the crescent tactic survived until the modern age. Requiring a high level of war analysis for that period, this tactic was especially successful against bulky armies. It was favored by mounted, swift-moving armies with light armor, such as Mongolian and Turkish armies, and the first close encounter was between troops at the center. After harsh clashes, these centrally located troops would withdraw en masse, and organized groups would encircle the enemy army that attempts to pursue them, creating a crescent shape. This strategy is predicated on pretending to escape to draw the enemy into an ambush and encircle them. The first users of the crescent strategy were the Scythians (Kafesioğlu, 1989). In the eighteenth century, this strategy was gradually replaced with European tactics (Çınar, 2014). This strategy has important similarities with the encirclement strategy, a basic military strategy.

Shock and Awe: Formalized by Ullman and Wade (1996), this doctrine is based on terrifying the enemy to destroy its will to fight with an overwhelming power. Shock and awe is based on the idea that excessive and sudden use of force (Bozkurt & Ergen/International Journal of Research in Business and Social Science) will scare and baffle the enemy. This strategy is more effective in frontal attacks. The counterpart of this strategy in marketing can be to conduct intense marketing communication with big budgets from many channels or sudden price reductions.

Blitzkrieg: Blitzkrieg is very similar to shock and awe (Ullman and Wade, 1996). The main military tactic of ponderous armies, it was used successfully in World War II by the Nazi army. This strategy seems more suitable for frontal attacks.

Discussion

The defensive and offensive strategies in the military literature have been adopted by the marketing literature as strategies that can be utilized by leader or challenger firms. Although there are not any studies on the relationship between some of the prominent models and approaches in the strategic marketing field and military strategies, there are some studies that refer to these concepts.

Product Life Cycle and the BCG Matrix: Coined by Joel Dean in 1950 and later developed by Levitt (1984), product life-cycle is the basis of many marketing studies. Based on the idea that products have a life cycle just like living things, the life cycle of a product consists of four stages: introduction, growth, maturity, and decline. A matrix developed by Boston Consulting Group in 1968 for portfolio analysis was a model for determining the market position of products and is parallel to product lifecycle strategies. In this matrix, products are categorized as question marks (during introduction to the market), stars (during growth), cash cows (during maturity), and dogs (during decline).

When strategies that can be utilized by firms in these areas are considered together with defensive and offensive strategies, we conclude that offensive strategies can be used during introduction and growth, defensive strategies can be used during maturity and defensive and withdrawal strategies can be used during decline.

Obviously, offensive strategies to be used during the introduction and growth periods will differ according to the competitive environment.

If there is no competition during the introduction period, the target of the attack will be customers rather than the competitors, the logical target if there is intense competition, basic competition factors, and generic strategies.

The terms *threat, battlefield,* and *competition* were used in 1980 by Michael Porter to talk about competition factors and to reflect on the relationship between marketing and military literature. The competitive environment shaped by competitors, suppliers, new entrances to the market, replacement products and threats from customers has similarities with the threats in a war situation.

The military strategies described in this study offer new perspectives and guidance to marketing managers in today's intense competitive conditions. There are other military strategies and tactics not included in this study and can be used by marketing experts. With the proliferation of interdisciplinary studies, military history and military strategies may be analyzed by marketing scholars with different perspectives. For some, in marketing warfare where the market is the battleground, competitors are enemies and CEO's are generals, traditional marketing weapons must be used more strategically. At this point, we believe that military literature can offer guidance to marketing experts. In further research, cyber warfare in military literature and digital marketing can be linked and researched.

PRINCIPLES OF SUN TZU & THE ART OF BUSINESS

1) Capture your market without destroying it

> "Generally in war, the best policy is to take a state intact; to ruin it is inferior to this....For to win one hundred victories in one hundred battles is not the acme of skill. To subdue the enemy without fighting is the acme of skill."
>
> — SUN TZU

Sun Tzu calls this the need to "win-all-without-fighting." Since the goal of your business is to survive and prosper, you must capture your market. However, you must do so in such a way that your market is not destroyed in the process. A company can do this in several ways, such as attacking parts of the market that are underserved or by using subtle, indirect, and low-key approaches that will not draw a competitor's attention or response. What should be avoided at all costs is a price-war. Research has shown that price attacks draw the quickest and most aggressive responses from competitors, as well as leaving the market drained of profits.

2) Avoid your competitor's strength, and attack their weakness

"An army may be likened to water, for just as flowing water avoids the heights and hastens to the lowlands, so an army avoids strength and strikes weakness."

— SUN TZU

The Western approach to warfare has spilled over into business competition, leading many companies to launch head-on, direct attacks against their competitor's strongest point. This approach to business strategy leads to battles of attrition, which end up being very costly for everyone involved. Instead, focus on the competition's weakness, which maximizes your gains while minimizing the use of resources. This, by definition, increases profits.

3) Use foreknowledge & deception to maximize the power of business intelligence.

"Know the enemy and know yourself; in a hundred battles, you will never be in peril."

— SUN TZU

To find and exploit your competitor's weakness requires a deep understanding of their executives' strategy, capabilities, thoughts, and desires, as well as similar depth of knowledge of your own strengths and weaknesses. Understand the overall competitive and industry trends around you to have a feel for the "terrain" on which you will do battle. Conversely, to keep your competitor from utilizing this strategy against you, it is critical to mask your plans and keep them secret.

4) Use speed and preparation to swiftly overcome the competition.

"To rely on rustics and not prepare is the greatest of crimes; to be prepared beforehand for any contingency is the greatest of virtues."

— SUN TZU

To exploit foreknowledge and deception, Sun Tzu states you must be able to act with blinding speed. To move with speed does not mean you do things hastily. In reality, speed requires much preparation. Reducing the time it takes your company to make decisions, develop products, and service customers is critical. To think through and understand potential competitive reactions to your attacks is essential.

5) Use alliances and strategic control points in the industry to "shape" your opponents and make them conform to your will.

"Therefore, those skilled in war bring the enemy to the field of battle and are not brought there by him."

— SUN TZU

"Shaping your competition" means changing the rules of contest and making the competition conform to your desires and your actions. It means taking control of the situation away from your competitor and putting it in your own hands. One way of doing so is through the skillful use of alliances. By building a strong web of alliances, the moves of your competitors can be limited. Also, by controlling key strategic points in your industry, you can play the tune to which your competitors dance.

6) Develop your character as a leader to maximize the potential of your employees.

"When one treats people with benevolence, justice, and righteousness, and reposes confidence in them, the army will be united in mind and all will be happy to serve their leaders."

— SUN TZU

It takes a special kind of leader to implement these strategic concepts and maximize the tremendous potential of employees. Sun Tzu describes the many traits of the preferred type of leader. The leader should be wise, sincere, humane, courageous, and strict. Leaders must also always be "first in the toils and fatigues of the army," putting their needs behind those of their troops. It is leaders with character that get the most out of their employees.

These principles have been utilized throughout time in both the military arena and the business world to build creative strategies and achieve lasting success. If you use them properly, they will bring you success.

7) Choose your battles

"He will win who knows when to fight and when not to fight."

— SUN TZU

As Sun Tzu argues armies should only engage when they have a clear advantage, we must pick our battles in real life. A child may fantasize about becoming a professional sports player, firefighter, CEO, and the president all at the same time, but as we get older, we realize there are time and resource constraints to what you can achieve. We should know what we can achieve and in which areas we will be most successful to take full advantage of the time and resources that are available. Sun Tzu recommends that military commanders avoid spreading their forces too thin, as that makes an army weaker throughout. Similarly, in your career, if you spread your skills over too many areas, you won't be able to specialize in anything. That is not to say having diverse skills won't help you get a job, but you have to diversify your skills in a smart way. In business, you must choose battles all the time, whether it be choosing between project proposals, prioritizing requests for renegotiations, or choosing when to challenge a counterpart. Much of content in *The Art of War* is dedicating to advising how to pick the right time and place for your conflict to occur (if it really must occur at all).

Sun Tzu's teachings can be applied to one's personal battles by helping us appreciate that self-improvement isn't just a matter of sheer willpower. When we have good habits we want to develop or bad habits we want to kick, it is helpful if we put ourselves in favorable conditions that will encourage success rather than make our challenges more difficult. For example, if you are trying to lose weight, eating out with friends while starting a diet will not help your case. Similarly, if you are trying to get a lot of reading done, loud and distracting housemates won't make that easy. Sun Tzu recommends following the path of least resistance. If you have multiple habits you want to build, start with the habits that are easiest to start, rather than trying to completely change your life all at once. Much like the feng shui tradition, Sun Tzu uses the metaphor of water flowing through the path of least resistance to describe the optimal course of action.

8) Timing is essential

"The quality of decision is like the well-timed swoop of a falcon which enables it to strike and destroy its victim."

— SUN TZU

Sun Tzu argues it is important to be prudent in choosing the timing of when to engage the enemy. While having a good strategy in mind is essential, a plan is only as good as it is appropriate for the situation. Having good timing means that while you do not hesitate to execute when the time is right, you don't rush in either unless the conditions favor it. In marketing, for example, pay attention to what is happening in a market before entering it, and to stay on top of trends, responding to them in real-time via social media like Twitter.

Sun Tzu knew that time was of the essence in warfare. In real life too, it is important that once a decision is made, it should be executed immediately. In the Chinese tech industry, for example, startups emphasize speed of execution and organizational flexibility to stay afloat. While China is a large market big enough to support many startups, it is generally considered a "winner take all" market, meaning that the first startups who succeed are likely to be the only ones that dominate.

9) Know yourself, know the enemy

"It is said that if you know your enemies and know yourself, you will not be imperiled in a hundred battles; if you do not know your enemies but do know yourself, you will win one and lose one; if you do not know your enemies nor yourself, you will be imperiled in every single battle."

— SUN TZU

Probably the most important point *The Art of War* tries to make is that information does matter, and an educated guess is better than a gut decision. Sun Tzu thought that generals should be adept at the "military calculus" of considering anything and everything that could affect the outcome of a battle. Not only is it vitally important to have insight into what the enemy might be attempting to do to take advantage of their weaknesses and know one's own corresponding strengths and weakness, but it is also important to consider factors such as the environment, weather, and troop morale. Recent trends in using big data demonstrate just how important in-depth research is to the survival and success of businesses. In business negotiations, knowing something about your counterpart can be vital to improving communication with them.

10) Have a unique plan

"All warfare is based on deception."

— SUN TZU

While this well-known quote from Sun Tzu's text sounds sinister, but it has profound meaning in the business world. It is essential to differentiate your business strategy to come out on top. The "military calculus" Sun wanted generals to be adept at was meant to incorporate one's own unique perspective, so that it would not be possible for the enemy to anticipate it. Similarly, if businesses do the same research as their rivals, the lack of differentiation would likely result in losing profits for both companies, as they would both be focusing on the same market areas. It is important in life's struggles to do the preparation work, but if you really want to win, prepare in a way that is either more extensive or more innovative than anyone else.

11) Disguise your plans

"When able to attack, we must seem unable; when using our forces, we must seem inactive; when we are near, we must make the enemy believe we are far away; when far away, we must make him believe we are near."

— SUN TZU

Sun Tzu believes it is not enough to have a unique plan, but that a plan must also be disguised with deception. For example, if a general was planning an attack from his left flank, he should confuse the enemy by using decoys on his right, which would make it appear as if the attack was coming from the right. Ideally, an army should also be in constant motion to appear formless. Deception is also common in the business world. Large corporate monopolies will often take measures to appear smaller, while small startups will claim they are changing the world through the uniqueness of their innovation, even though they might not be at that stage yet. Similarly, if your ambition is to leave your current company to start your own business in the same industry, you would do well to have your colleagues believe you depend on your job. Sun Tzu also recommends that you make your former colleagues think your performance is struggling until you eventually reach the point where you are outperforming them.

12) The best way to win is to not fight at all

"To win one hundred battles is not the height of skill, to subdue the enemy without fighting is."

— SUN TZU

In observation that warfare is risky, Sun Tzu proposes that the best tacticians are those who can defeat the enemy by diplomacy or other means. He proposed generals should try to take cities without laying siege, possibly by forcing the inhabitants to surrender via psychological warfare. Sun Tzu argues that for any situation, man has more than one tool at his disposal, making it sometimes necessary to engage the enemy in a conventional manner. The concept of being resourceful applies to real life even more than it does to military conflict, as not a zero-sum game, and there can be multiple winners. The example of Apple's "Think Different" campaign illustrates how companies can become successful not by direct competition, but by differentiation. Similarly, in personal life, you are much more likely to succeed if you create your own job opportunities than if you follow normal, more established career paths.

Develop a skill (or combination of skills) nobody else has, and you won't have to compete with anyone. Want to get hired? Figuring out how to get companies to seek you out rather than you having to seek them out will save you a lot of time and effort.

13) Change represents opportunity

"In the midst of chaos, there is opportunity."

— SUN TZU

According to Sun Tzu, change is one of the most important factors in deciding the outcome of a battle. As a realist, Sun Tzu emphasizes that anything can happen in warfare, and proposing that generals always prepare for the worst. However, he also points out that the only way to get ahead is to take the right risks. Therefore, those who remain calm and keep an open mind during a time of uncertainty are best-positioned to take advantage of opportunities when they arise. In real life and in business, often one is unaware of the opportunities one has missed because people are so often fixated on protecting themselves from change. Change is inevitable in any industry, and the best way to prepare for change is to be the driving force behind that change. Being aware of new laws or regulations, disruptive technologies, social phenomena, and changes in the budget of your customers will uncover opportunities, which must be seized if businesses are to progress.

14) Success breeds success

"Opportunities multiply as they are seized."

— SUN TZU

Sun Tzu noticed that momentum was very important to warfare. The same is true in business. When Uber was vying for market dominance with local ride-hailing app Didi Dache (Dīdī

Dǎchē), Uber was the clear favorite as a more technologically advanced and better-funded startup. CEO of Didi, Cheng Wei, reportedly a military history buff, told Uber CEO Travis Kalanick he would someday overtake Uber when the two met in 2013. Although he was at the time much smaller than Uber, Cheng knew he would someday win, because he was going to have to fight other local ride-hailing apps before he challenged Uber anyway. After defeating or acquiring all the local rivals, Didi had become a seasoned veteran in the Chinese market and knew how to fight much better than Uber, a U.S.-based company. Cheng's string of victories against local rivals eventually helped him outmaneuver Uber, despite Uber's ability to match his moves financially. Companies like Didi can scale quickly once they have a few successes, and the momentum shifts their way. Similarly, in a career, sometimes the small actions snowball into something bigger. For example, if you volunteer to represent your company at a conference, it could lead to networking great contacts who give you clients, or a future job. Sometimes, it just takes one opportunity for the floodgates to open.

15) No one profits from prolonged warfare

"There is no instance of a nation benefiting from prolonged warfare."

— SUN TZU

Uber and Didi can attest to the draining effects of a protracted conflict, as both companies burned through billions of dollars while competing with one another. Sun Tzu advises it is best to strike effectively and quickly, making conflict decisive. In the business world, you don't want to drain your resources attacking a rival when you could invest them in your future development. In personal life too, you do not want to wait forever to tackle your problems and should make progress toward your goals as soon as possible. Do you have an idea to start an innovative company? Don't wait until next year to get things rolling, as someone else with the same idea might act on it sooner than you.

PRODUCTIVITY AND THE ART OF WAR:

APPLYING SUN TZU'S TEACHINGS TO BUSINESS

How can we apply Sun Tzu's principles of warfare to our modern goals for productivity?

1. PERSONAL ACCOUNTABILITY

Sun Tzu said: "If words of command are not clear and distinct, if orders are not thoroughly understood, then the general is to blame."

The Bottom Line: If you communicate ineffectively, then any problems caused by unclear communication are your fault. Make sure that every email and conversation you have is clear and distinct.

The important corollary to this aphorism is important to remember as well: "But if his orders ARE clear, and the soldiers nevertheless disobey, then it is the fault of their officers." If other people are hampering your productivity, take decisive action.

2. KEEPING YOUR COOL

Sun Tzu said: "Disciplined and calm, to await the appearance of disorder and hubbub amongst the enemy–this is the art of retaining self-possession."

The Bottom Line: The fastest way to lose productivity is to lose your cool. Take a deep breath and think before acting rashly. If you can keep your wits about you in the midst of a crisis, it will serve you well.

An important quote that relates to this concept is: "Do not swallow bait offered by the enemy. Do not interfere with an army that is returning home." Staying productive and staying professional are the same. Never lose your cool with coworkers or bosses. At least, not where it can get back to them.

3. BE PREPARED

Sun Tzu said: "The art of war teaches us to rely not on the likelihood of the enemy's not coming, but on our own readiness to receive him; not on the chance of his not attacking, but rather on the fact that we have made our position unassailable."

The Bottom Line: Do everything in your power to be prepared because it's only a matter of time until something goes wrong. If you have daily deadlines, work two days ahead to give yourself a buffer. Take initiative to track trends in your division, so that when your boss asks you to compile a report, the work is already done. Think of all the possible complications you might have to contend with and work out a plan to be ready for when the inevitable happens.

4. DO WORK TO GET WORK

Sun Tzu said: "Opportunities multiply as they are seized."

The Bottom Line: The boss needs volunteers to stay late and work on a project? Do it. Your company needs a speaker to represent them at a conference? Do it. The more experience you gain, the better your resume will look, and the higher the quality of your contacts will be.

Just be careful of spreading yourself too thin.

5. GROW YOUR SOCIAL NETWORK

Sun Tzu said: "Tactics without strategy is the noise before defeat. Strategy without tactics is the slowest route to victory."

The Bottom Line: Stay in touch with former co-workers, colleagues, and yes, even bosses. You never know when a former business contact may recommend you for a new position. But it's not enough to just stay in touch. You must have a plan for how you can leverage your connections.

Note: This quote, while attributed to Sun Tzu, is likely apocryphal.

Nonetheless, it is good advice.

6. BE SELFLESS

Sun Tzu said: "The general who advances without coveting fame and retreats without fearing disgrace, whose only thought is to protect his country and do good service for his sovereign, is the jewel of the kingdom."

The Bottom Line: No one likes a manipulative ladder-climber. Just do what is best for the company, and ultimately, you'll be doing what's best for you, too. Stay humble, even after winning awards and accolades, and you'll make more friends (read: allies).

7. PLAY TO YOUR STRENGTHS

Sun Tzu said: "It is said that if you know your enemies and know yourself, you will not be imperiled in a hundred battles; if you do not know your enemies but do know yourself, you will win one and lose one; if you do not know your enemies nor yourself, you will be imperiled in every single battle."

The Bottom Line: If you always play to your personal strengths and understand any potential problems that could cause a decline in your productivity, you will always succeed in your industry. Stay abreast of industry trends, and always keep honing your skill set.

Sun Tzu may have been the master of wartime strategies, but his advice still resonates with us today because it can be so readily applied to politics, business, and our personal lives. Follow his precepts, and everything will go your way.

MORE POWERFUL STRATEGIES ON POWERFUL STRATEGY AND BUSINESS:

FIVE ESSENTIALS FOR VICTORY

1. He will win who knows when to fight and when not to fight.

The general, who is adept at winning, understands that supreme excellence is not about fighting and conquering in all your battles but that it is about breaking the enemy's resistance without fighting. The general adept at selecting the right battles and fighting the battles right through variations of tactics and troops will lead to victory. The general who does not understand this may not be able to turn his knowledge to practical account and will fail to make the best use of his men.

Case in Point: In the business world, it's not always about the win-lose game between you and your competition; you can help maintain or increase the overall industry and market size; you can define your niche or partner with other industry players to grow your business without destroying the market. Win-Win game is possible in business.

2. He will win who knows how to handle both superior and inferior forces.

Leadership is a matter of humaneness, trustworthiness, wisdom, courage, sincerity, benevolence, intelligence, and discipline. Discipline means organization, chain of command, and logistics. For marshaling of the army, discipline must be understood in its proper subdivisions, the graduations of rank among the officers, the control of expenditure, and the maintenance of roads for supplies to the army. A wise leader will effectively blend advantages and disadvantages together in his plans and will compare the military conditions of its opponent(s) using following seven considerations. With these seven considerations, one can forecast victory or defeat.

Moral law – in which army does it pervade the most?

- Ability - which of the two generals is most able?
  Advantage – which army has the most advantage
  (speed) derived from Heaven (sky) and Earth?
- Discipline – which army rigorously enforces discipline
  the most?
- Strength – which army is stronger?
- Training and Competency – which army highly trains
  their officers and men?
- Reward and Punishment – which army exemplifies
  greater consistency in both?

The general who understands and masters the importance of these seven considerations will reach the victory without lengthy operations in the field. The consummate leader cultivates the moral law, and strictly adheres to method and discipline; thus, he can control outcome and success. Such generals should be retained in command. While these seven considerations are important, one should employ and leverage all helpful resources and circumstances over and beyond the ordinary rules.

Case in Point: To drive the right behaviors and results, *strategic and adaptive leadership* is critical, whether in business, sports or military. As management guru Peter Drucker says, "Only three things happen naturally in organizations: friction, confusion, and underperformance.

Everything else requires leadership. Whenever you see a successful business or outcome, someone once made a courageous decision. Effective leadership is not about making speeches or being liked; leadership is defined by results, not attributes. Leadership is not about flattering, manipulating and being popular. Leadership is lifting a person's vision to higher sights, the raising of a person's performance to a higher standard, the building of a personality beyond its normal limitations. Regarding future, the only thing we know about the future is that it will be different and the best way to predict the future is to create it."

3. He will win whose army is animated by the same spirit throughout all its ranks.

A winning army will have all its officers and men imbued with the same spirit throughout all its ranks. The general, without fear and with only desire to protect and serve his country, who advances without coveting fame and retreats without fearing disgrace, is the jewel of the kingdom or his country.

There are three ways a ruler or general can bring misfortune upon his army:

By employing the officers without qualification or ability and through ignorance of the military principle of adaptation to circumstances. If the general employs or promotes unqualified "Yes Men" as officers, soldiers will lose confidence and faith in the institution.

By being ignorant, his army may not be in condition to obey his orders. This causes more damage than any benefits or advantage.

By being ignorant of the army operating conditions and methods and trying to administer it like a kingdom, the commander causes restlessness in the soldiers' minds.

The general may be infected with five dangerous faults he must avoid:

Cowardice, which leads to capture

Ruthlessness, which leads to careless destruction

Short temper, which can be provoked

Desire for honor, which is sensitive to shame

Over-solicitude for his men, which leads to trouble

Case in Point: Leadership is a privilege; it is about nurturing and enhancing. As a leader, your job is to take charge of your own energy and then help to orchestrate the energy of those around you. Your team and their behaviors will reflect you, you must live and breathe the vision and values you expect to see in others. Develop your character as a leader to maximize the potential of your employees. Leading your people at whim, throwing tantrums, bullying, being insensitive to their core values, and protecting mediocrity will lead into trouble. Whether you're a big company or a start-up, people are the only real assets you have. Customers will not love the company unless employees love it; your employees are your brand ambassadors to customers.

Steve Jobs is often quoted as saying "A players hire B players; B players hire C players, and C players hire D players. It doesn't take long to get to Z players. This trickle-down effect causes bozo explosions in companies."

4. He will win who, prepared himself, waits to take the enemy unprepared.

"All men see the tactics whereby I conquer, but none see the strategy out of which victory is evolved. Tactics without strategy are the noise before defeat. Strategy without tactics is the slowest route to victory. Therefore, to be victorious you need prepare both Strategy and Tactics for deployment. The victorious strategist only seeks battle after the victory has been won, whereas he who is destined to defeat first fights and afterwards looks for victory." –Sun Tzu

The general should avoid repeating the same old tactics that delivered victory previously and regulate the use of these tactical methods by accounting for an infinite variety of circumstances. Military tactics should be like water; water shapes its natural course according to the nature of the ground over which it flows and it runs downwards from high to low places. So, in war, the general adapts to the warfare situations and works out his victory in relation to the opponent he is facing, while avoiding his opponent's strengths and striking the weaknesses.

The general who can modify his tactics in relation to his opponent will win. Therefore, it is said,

- If you know your enemies and know yourself, you will not be imperiled in a hundred battles.
- If you do not know your enemies but know yourself, you will win one and lose one.
- If you do not know your enemies nor yourself, you will be imperiled in every single battle.

The skillful fighters first put themselves beyond the possibility of defeat, then wait for an opportunity to defeat the enemy. So, they do not rely on the likelihood of the enemy's not coming or chance of his not attacking, but on their own readiness to receive him and making their own position invincible. Whoever is first in the field and waits for opponent's arrival will be fresh for the fight; whoever comes second to the field will arrive exhausted and has to hasten to battle.

To see victory only when it is within the ken of the common herd is not the acme of excellence. Neither is it the acme of excellence if you fight and conquer and the whole Empire says, "Well done!" To lift an autumn hair is no sign of great strength; to see the sun and moon is no sign of sharp sight; to hear the noise of thunder is no sign of a quick ear. What the ancients called a clever fighter is one who not only wins but excels in winning with ease. Hence his victories bring him neither reputation for wisdom nor credit for courage. He wins his battles by making no mistakes. Making no mistakes establishes the certainty of victory, for it means conquering an enemy already defeated.

Case in Point: The best way to predict the future is to create it. To create your future, you must prepare yourself and seize the opportunity when it shows up. If you're an entrepreneur, you may even create the opportunity that doesn't exist; you may find order in disorder and clarity in chaos. As a business leader, know your industry and know your unique place and position in that industry. While you analyze the past, deliver the present and plan for future, prepare for disruptive innovation and threat from players outside of your industry.

If you need examples, you need not search too hard:

Airbnb, the world's largest accommodation provider, owns no real estate and it is disrupting the hotel industry.

Uber, the world's largest taxi company, owns no vehicles and it is disrupting the taxi industry.

Facbook, the world's most popular social networking and media owner, creates no content. It killed its competition, Myspace, and Orkut.

Alibaba, the most valuable retailer, has no inventory and it is disrupting the Chinese retail industry. It even has the potential to disrupt US e-commerce.

Netflix, the biggest online entertainer, originally owned no media content and it disrupted Blockbuster, DVD rentals, then TV production, and now films.

Apple changed the game of five industries with the iFamily – iPad, iPod, iPhone, iTunes, and more. Steve Jobs affected and changed five industries forever - personal computing, animation, music, phones, and mobile computing.

LinkedIn, the world's most popular professional networking site is disrupting corporate recruitment industry and business infor-mation/training industry.

5. He will win who has military capacity and is not interfered with by the sovereign.

Underlying advantage of war is speed and unique military strengths, which helps take advantage of opponent's unreadiness by traveling uncharted territories and routes. The army is to be managed with one principle, and that is to set up one standard of courage which all soldiers must reach. Hence, the skillful leader tailors his approach to his men and leads his army just as though he were leading a single soldier, by the hand and considering his strengths and weaknesses.

No more than seven musical notes exist, yet their combinations yield more melodies than can ever be heard. No more three five primary colors (blue, yellow, and red) exist, yet their combinations yield more colors than can ever be seen. No more than four cardinal tastes (sour, salty, sweet, bitter) exist, yet their combinations yield more flavors than can ever be tasted. In warfare, two methods of attack exist - the direct and the indirect; yet their combination yields endless series of maneuvers. It is like moving in a circle, where you never come to an end. The quality of decision is equally critical – a quality decision is like the well-timed stroke of the hammer to destroy the crisis situation and emerge victorious. Therefore, a seasoned fighter will be prompt in his decision, as he understands that speed is an advantage. Let your rapidity be that of the wind; your compactness that of the forest; your immovability like a mountain; your plans dark and impenetrable as night, and when you move, fall like a thunderbolt. Such is the art of maneuvering.

Amidst confusion and chaos, turmoil and disorder, you will find the proof against defeat to succeed in victory. Ponder and deliberate before you make every move. Simulated disorder postulates perfect discipline, simulated fear postulates courage; simulated weakness postulates strength.

In military method, there are five elements:
Measurement
Estimation of quantity
Calculation
Balancing of chances
Victory

To succeed in victory, the general must balance chances; to balance chances, he needs calculation; to calculate, he must estimate quantity; to estimate quantity, he must measure; to measure, he must assess earth and sky (competitive landscape) with local guides.

The consummate leaders first make their army invincible because that's what they can control, and they watch for vulnerability in their opponents, as they cannot cause opponents to be vulnerable. Therefore, a victorious army first wins, and only then seeks battle; a defeated army first battles then seeks victory.

The victorious business leaders, athletes, or entrepreneurs perceive opportunity in crisis when others don't; they believe in their team and strengths when others don't; they first make themselves invincible; they learn to adapt and conquer uncertainty. They leverage all sort of intelligence and facts to balance chances. They multiply their opportunities by seizing them. They master the fundamentals and move fast compared to their competition.

In summary:

Regardless of business, sports, or military – successes of the most successful companies, start-ups, athletes, and leaders is not a matter of luck or an accident but an outcome of consistently mastering the essentials, whether some call it "The Art of War," "The Art of Strategy," or "The Art of Winning." It takes focus, hard work, sacrifice, learning, studying, and most importantly, loving what you're doing. Outsiders typically see it as overnight victory or luck. Gary Player, one of the greatest players in the history of golf, once said, "The harder you work, the luckier you get."

SELLING STRATEGIES LEARNED FROM THE ART OF WAR

Today's challenging economy requires sales organizations to consider new ways to sell. In every technology company, Sales must work with development, product management, and marketing to identify key product attributes. More importantly, sales must have a clear understanding of the business value they provide. To illustrate the selling strategy, let's equate them to the strategies in Sun Tzu's *The Art of War*.

IN HIS BOOK, TZU IDENTIFIES THE 5 STRATEGIES AS FOLLOWS:

- **Direct**
- **Indirect**
- **Divisional**
- **Contain**
- **Delay**

Strategies 1 and 2 are action-oriented strategies and directly applicable to discussion of selling strategies. Most technology company's sales organizations use a Direct Strategy, the de facto strategy of choice. A Direct Strategy focuses on selling tools or technology to customers, but not business value. A few years ago, Spatial recognized that the Direct Strategy did not enable our customers to readily see the value of our products. Spatial now uses an Indirect Strategy to meet our sales objectives with an emphasis on a Value Selling Model as a consulting tool. Spatial adopted the Value Selling Model five years ago and has experienced higher sales growth and customer retention ever since.

Value Selling improves our ability to articulate our business value vs. our previous method of selling what the technology does. With this selling strategy, Spatial has:

- Shortened sales cycles
- Increased revenue streams with improved profitability
- Reached mutually-favorable contracts with our customers
- Increased effectiveness in selling into new markets
- Increased our portfolio of products with existing customers

WHAT'S BEST: DIRECT OR INDIRECT SELLING STRATEGIES?

Rapidly changing technology coupled with ever-changing customer demands make technology selling propositions expensive and risky. For example; Direct Selling strategies require that the seller have at least a 3:1 advantage over a competitor to win. This 3:1 advantage is usually achieved by selling product attributes such as price, performance, and product features. Value Selling, however, promotes articulating and delivering provable, repeatable value to the customer and sustains a far more profitable business with more meaningful partnerships.

In our sales terminology, aligning our value with our customers is striving to be a "Conscious Competent." With a Conscious Competent model, the salesperson understands the keys to their success and can define the value they bring. Conversely, the "Unconscious Competent" refers to seemingly successful salespeople that sell high volumes with "hot" products, in new markets, with high demand, or with limited competition. This success masks the need for a defined selling model - the desire to have a methodology that is "conscious" and successful.

To succeed, our Sales organization works with our customers to define their business objectives, therefore building lasting, impenetrable, and mutually profitable business relationships. With that both Spatial and our customer's win. And your organization can too if you choose the right selling strategy and practice the art of war.

MASTER BUSINESS STRATEGY WITH 13 TACTICS FROM THE ART OF WAR

THE LAYING OF PLANS, CALCULATIONS, AND ESTIMATIONS

The book states: before any steps are taken, research and planning are the keys to any venture. The Interpretation? Any blueprint or business plan must be compiled with reference to five basic points:

- Seasonal Factors and Timing
- Landscape or Operational Terrain
- Leadership Qualities – wisdom, sincerity, benevolence, courage, and strictness
- Management Skills – covering logistics, methodology and organizational structure
- Moral Law – the way of the world and the laws of human nature.

This strategy handbook proceeds to lay out seven methods for forecasting based on your capabilities these factors. It calls for a SWOT Analysis.

Here, it also calls for leaders to adhere to classic principles in

Project Management. It advises you to have awareness of your capabilities and surroundings, adjust your plans to suit your resources and track or monitor your operations against possible deviation from the original plan. Get back on track quickly, he says.

Once plans are in operation, we must outwit our competition by not betraying our course and be subtle in our direction. One of the most succinct quotes from this treatise says:

"All warfare is based on deception."

Waging War – The Challenge

The next segment focuses on the importance of decisive behavior, correct timing, and economy in your actions. Before embarking in any ventures, we can minimize challenges, conflict and ensuing costs by:

Focusing on the logistics of any plan and prevent over-extension of your company's resources.

Maintaining organizational morale and keeping the "Troops" motivated and well resourced.

Sun Tzu provides us with a clever tip – If you are low on resources and want to save: focus more on exploiting your competitor's weakness rather than throwing more cash/resources at the problem.

Consider the wisdom of having effective exit strategies in place if something does not work.

"Let your main object be victory, not lengthy drawn-out campaigns."

Attack by Stratagem or Planning Offensives

Here Sun Tzu echoes that adage, it's not size but unity that determines strength and organizational effectiveness. He makes that now famous quote:

> "The skillful leader subdues the enemy's troops without any fighting."

In other words, avoid competing head on and avoid using up resources directly against competitors. Aim instead for excellence, so that no other organization would even dare compete. Create a natural monopoly.

How?

In a business environment, it's being interpreted as taking the initiative and being first to market or innovate. Engage a pre-emptive "attack" on your competitors with your superior offering thus demotivating any would-be contenders with your superior market share. Invent the most innovative product, process, occupy new territory or be the first to secure the marketplace.

Failing that, "Surround them," assuming you have adequate resources to cover the market and try for a Me-too approach.

If you have insufficient resources, a divide and conquer approach may work. Segment the market or break your problem into parts and attack each individually.

Failing that – your only option is to meet your (enemy) competitor head on. In business terms, I interpret this as a potential Price war.

Failing that, you will be forced into a siege mentality which is costly for both attacker and the attacked.

Once you run out of resources, you will have to retreat or drop out of the market – become the victim of shake-out.

Sun Tzu also points out ways you can damage things as a leader:

Having an insufficient vision and a poor overview of the situation. This results in using the incorrect resources or methods to meet the right challenges.

Not being decisive or flexible enough to exploit opportunities- not knowing when to act/when not to act.

Running an organization without the means to respond to your directives and isn't able to act on its own initiative when required. Recruiting of decisive and strong management is essential here.

Conversely, not communicating your goals clearly and leaving your team to their own devices – the mark of a poor leader with an undisciplined team.

Poor human resource management skills that utilize the wrong people for the wrong task, the inability to motivate your team or facilitate it.

In other words:

"If you know neither the enemy nor yourself, you will succumb in every battle."

Tactical Dispositions or Positioning

This phase of his treatise emphasizes defensive behavior: securing and consolidating the resources you have and using them effectively as a solid base for exploiting new opportunities when they occur. This is a reminder to business to get your housekeeping in order, be efficient and lean cost-wise. Have insurance or fail-safes before embarking on anything new or risky.

"One may KNOW how to conquer without being able to DO it."

Energy & Direction

This subtopic is about capturing momentum and synergy.

"The quality of decision is like the well-timed swoop of a falcon which enables it to strike and destroy its victim."

Sun Tzu outlines direct and indirect/subtle methods of accomplishing your mission—let us call them obvious versus not-so-obvious, downright sneaky methods. He encourages us to use these two approaches creatively and in tandem.

Being able to alternate methods generates momentum and ensures sustainable results.

Tips on how to "win" the battle include:

- The element of surprise
- Deception
- Masking your true strength when trying to outflank or outwit your "opponent"
- Using Bait to outwit your opponents and draw their true intentions and positions
- Not relying on any one person but instead focusing on the
- discipline and unity of your team business strategy

Weak Points and Strong/Illusion versus Reality

Here Sun Tzu helps us spot the best opportunities for attack, how to spot weaknesses in your opponent and position yourself in the most advantageous way. In business terms, this can be interpreted in his advice as follows:

- Take the initiative rather than play catch up – you may waste more resources playing catch up than in taking entrepreneurial risks.
- Be aware of your Competition's weak points, expose them and hasten to do better in these areas quickly.
- Be aware of markets or territories where your Competitor has no presence and exploit these gaps.
- Be aware of Competitive advantage. Maximize your resources where you possess natural barriers to entry.
- Be a moving target and make it hard for your Competitors to guess your next move.
- Never overextend yourself and focus on your Core Competencies.

If you have weak organizational flaws, consolidate your resources in strengthening a few critical areas, not all of them at once. Timing is everything– research the best moment in which to activate your plans.

> "Do not repeat the tactics which have gained you one victory, but let your methods be regulated by the infinite variety of circumstances."

Maneuvering and Dealing with Direct Conflict

Sometimes, we must still meet difficult challenges head on and may not circumvent them. Sun Tzu advises us to maintain the following if we are to emerge unscathed and maximize our tactical advantage.

KEY NOTES HERE ARE:

Personnel – Maintain harmonious relationships between all levels of your hierarchy and create a unity within your organization that operates to an internal discipline. Ensure they get a share of the "spoils" to keep them motivated and help them buy into the company mission.

Logistics – Always ensure clear lines of supply secured to sustain you throughout your campaign.

Local Knowledge – Make sure you have good local knowledge of your market, with an insider's view.

Competition – Know when they are operating at peak strength and only launch your attack when you know they are recovering from another campaign or when they are on downtime.

Do not enter into an alliance until you are certain of the motives of your partners.

"The difficulty of tactical maneuvering consists in turning the devious into the direct, and misfortune into gain."

Variation in Tactics a.k.a. the Innumerable Changes

This section talks about the art of judgment. Good tactics also mean knowing what NOT to do. It is not enough to know your business and environment well; you also need versatility of mind.

In business terms, this is being interpreted as knowing what paths not to follow, markets that are not worth pursuing or contracts and alliances that are a no-win for your business.

If subordinate to a higher command, Sun Tzu implies there are situations where you must not even obey your superiors. You could even say it may be a good thing to flout conventional wisdom.

In everything you do, always have the versatility of mind to inhabit the thinking behind competitors or customers' actions.

Take a 360-degree approach to everything you do and be mindful of all your stakeholders in any action you take, this allows you to escape hidden pitfalls or exploit every potential advantage/opportunity not just obvious ones. The sort of thinking can be found in guerrilla marketing approaches or CSR marketing that exploits nonobvious opportunities.

"In the midst of difficulties we are always ready to seize an advantage, we may extricate ourselves from misfortune."

The Army on the March/Moving the Force

This segment focuses on observing the right signs in your "enemy." This can be interpreted as the ability to read your environment correctly and forecast effectively based on the behavior of your competitors, economy, potential customers and even stakeholders. He details clever practical tips for reading your enemy's behavior on the battlefield.

A great leader can read the signs around him, track history, and therefore be alert to deception or sudden changes by correctly extrapolating future behavior.

He gives an acute reading of human behavior below:

"When envoys are sent with compliments in their mouths, it is a sign that the enemy wishes for a truce."

Terrain or Situational Positioning

In anything we do – we will encounter points of resistance. How we position ourselves may cause assorted advantages and disadvantages. In the original text, he inventories the geographical terrains an ancient army may encounter and prescribes the best positions to take.

Sun Tzu emphasizes:

A Point of Vantage. Make sure that no matter where you are, you have a clear view of the endgame.

Sneaky Tip 1: When no one makes the first move or you don't know where your competitor is, do a false retreat to draw out your prospective opponents.

Sneaky Tip 2: If your competitor has a superior position to you, entice them to focus on something else and fool them into vacating their no.1 spot

Secure Lines of supply and good Communications throughout your organization are essential, otherwise, there will be a disconnect between your best-laid plans and execution on the ground.

Find yourself trying to match up to your competitor and always trailing behind? Taoism can be a destructive activity that eats up too many resources. Reconsider the campaign in the first place.

Six signs to show you are failing as a leader

Flight: when you put your organization against a superior force with no preparation

Insubordination: when management is weak and discipline falls apart

Collapse: when workers are under-resourced

Ruin: when Management does not buy into the organizational mission and rebels

Disorganization: when there are no clear organizational rules, roles, or best practice laid down

Rout: when the wrong resources or tactics are being used.

> "The power of estimating the adversary, of controlling the forces of victory, and of shrewdly calculating difficulties, dangers and distances, constitutes the test of a great general."

The Nine Situations/Terrains

According to Sun Tzu, there are nine common stages in any campaign. He prescribes reactions to each one in terms of old world battle scenarios. Some prescriptions are obvious...

On home ground: don't waste too many resources campaigning here.

On entering new territory: keep pushing aggressively early in the campaign if nothing gets in the way, and as long as you have a clear, easy exit strategy. You aren't too heavily invested at this stage and can turn back if need be.

Contentious ground or strategically essential territory: do not be the first to move without smoking out your competitors' intentions first and understanding their strategy too. Hide your true interests and distract the competition where possible from discovering them.

Open ground or easily accessible territory: don't hinder other competitors by assuming their activity is of no strategic relevance to your mission.

Ground of Intersecting Highways, where there is activity from more than one interested party or contender: form alliances with others.

Serious ground, where much effort was required to secure this territory and you are in a precarious position: it may be hard to exit and hard to move forward. A "Winning Hearts and Minds" policy is required here. Do not antagonize any stakeholders and do your best to sustain all of your business relationships at their optimum levels.

Difficult ground or difficult conditions in which to operate: keep going and don't stop until you are in a safer position. In business terms, I interpret this as consolidating resources, being cost-conscious, and keeping your productivity high, maintaining and pushing for higher targets.

Hemmed-in ground, where it is difficult to extricate oneself from this situation: resort to deception, intrigue, and stratagem.

Desperate ground, where there is no exit possible: once there, you must stick it out and give it everything you've got, it's all about survival.

Sun Tzu compares a skillful tactician to a species of mountain snake, due to his ability to react quickly:

> "Strike at its head, and you will be attacked by its tail; strike at its tail, and you will be attacked by its head; strike at its middle, and you will be attacked by head and tail both."

The Attack by Fire

This next segment seems a little esoteric, especially if trying to apply to contemporary business models – Sun Tzu talks about five ways to attack by fire. But it is a reminder of the strategic ways a person can mount an offensive campaign to any competitor (from the inside).

The Soldiers – Poach their personnel, demotivate them or use them?

The Stores – Attack your competitors' financial investments?

The Baggage Trains – Their logistics, lines of supply, or key suppliers?

The Arsenal and Magazines – Attack your competitors cash-cows and sources of revenue?

Hurl fire On Your Enemy as Artillery – Attack their operations, throw a spanner in the works?

Most important – Follow up the internal attack with your own offensive on the outside and be resourced, time it right, and don't get caught up in the fire.

"Unhappy is the fate of one who tries to win his battles and succeed in his attacks without cultivating the spirit of enterprise; for the result is waste of time and general stagnation."

The Use of Spies/Intelligence

Sun Tzu warns us against wasteful campaigns that expend a lot of resources or hours of labor when a simple use of intelligence or Foreknowledge would be more efficient.

According to the text, it can only be obtained through scout masters, reconnaissance, or five kinds of spies:

Local spies

Inward spies

Converted spies

Doomed spies

Surviving spies

The main points here are:

Reward your spies liberally and be sagacious yet sincere when dealing with them. Above all, keep this operation in utmost secrecy internally.

If you wish to convert someone into a spy – spoil them. A converted spy is your greatest asset, as they can help you recruit more.

Spies are a most important element in water because on them depends an army's ability to move.

MORE ON GREAT BUSINESS PRINCIPLES
FROM THE ART OF WAR

All armies prefer high ground to low and sunny places to dark.

The metaphorical synergy here is obvious, but perhaps not to all. People continually try to reinvent the wheel and often refuse to let go. It's a choice on what you are to tackle, but market research, intelligence, and analysis should be first and foremost. On the flip side, competition is a good thing.

> "All men can see the tactics whereby I conquer, but what none can see is the strategy out of which victory is evolved."

Everyone is trying to create a form of reselling success.

It's hard work, luck and having oneself ready for opportunity. Individuals in ways will and should develop tactics discovered from personal successes and failures. Gerald Loeb has a famous quote, of which is used often, and it went along the lines of:

> "Listen to everyone, follow no one."

When the enemy is close at hand and remains quiet, he is relying on the natural strength of his position.

This covers high-frequency traders and even server positions close to Twitter's data center, etc. Is it that business hubs are created to feed off each other? Of course, but enemies back then differed from enemies now, in some respects. A business wishing to grab market share from an opponent should be as close to that opponent as they can, either through intelligence, surveillance, or being physically close to them.

Ponder and deliberate before you make a move. Research and think, hard.

"He, who can modify his tactics in relations to his opponent and thereby succeed in winning, may be called a heaven-born captain."

I would suggest applying this to your tactics and center in on success because if you take anything from this, for all that is known all champions may be going to Valhalla. This is all about pivoting.

THE BEST MANAGEMENT ADVICE FROM "THE ART OF WAR"

"A wise general makes a point of foraging on the enemy. One cartload of the enemy's provisions is equivalent to twenty of one's own, and likewise a single picul of his provender is equivalent to twenty from one's own store."

This sentiment is pretty much universally applicable to business. Something obtained cheaply or for free is vastly more valuable than drawing from company cash or savings to buy it. In practice, that means both looking for things underpriced and having funds available when demand and prices are low.

"When you engage in actual fighting, if victory is long in coming, then men's weapons will grow dull and their ardor will be damped. If you lay siege to a town, you will exhaust your strength."

This is a concept that's repeated several times. When a project or initiative takes too long, people get tired or bored, the competition knows too much about it, it gets outdated, and other companies or people take advantage.

"To see victory only when it is within the ken of the common herd is not the acme of excellence."

A strategy, product, or concept that is obvious has probably already been done. Those that are the best succeed without people really noticing. They not only become part of the fabric of people's lives, they're also not as easily replicated.

"The clever combatant looks to the effect of combined energy, and does not require too much from individuals. Hence his ability to pick out the right men and utilize combined energy."

Another axiom in the book compares using combined energy to rolling logs or stones. People moving together with momentum go dramatically faster. Depending on individuals alone means they'll wear out, accomplish less, and leave other people behind.

"If you order your men to roll up their buff-coats, and make forced marches without halting day or night, covering double the usual distance at a stretch, doing a hundred LI in order to wrest an advantage, the leaders of all your three divisions will fall into the hands of the enemy."

Here, a "Li" equals five-hundred meters. Tzu says that if you do something like this, the strongest men will be in front, the less motivated will fall behind, and a tiny fraction will reach their destination. Pushing incredibly hard to get ahead of a competitor might gain temporary advantage, but it will be very short-lived.

COMPETITOR ANALYSIS STRATEGIES FROM THE ART OF WAR

LEARN WHO YOUR TRUE COMPETITORS ARE

Many companies assume they know their competition, which isn't surprising if they have been in business for a long time. However, this can be a dangerous assumption. Traditionally, the competition is defined from the company perspective, not from the perspective of your customers. Your customers, however, will ultimately determine your true competitors, not your strategy team. Conducting a competitor analysis through the eyes of your customers will ensure that you are benchmarking yourself correctly.

DETERMINE YOUR COMPETITION'S STRATEGY

Even though the level of competition online has continued to increase since the digital age, one thing in your company's favor is that your competition is constantly broadcasting their marketing strategy on their website. For example, if lead generation is the goal of their website, you will see lots of offers for gated content "locked" behind forms. If they are using a content marketing strategy, you'll likely see a well-trafficked blog with sharable content. Nothing is secret anymore. From the language they use to attract their target markets (or buyer personas) to the way they expect visitors to flow through their website, it is all out in the open for anyone to see. You get to experience how prospects move through the buyer's journey. This can give you powerful insight into how your competitors are positioning themselves, as well as where their strengths and weaknesses lie.

STUDY WHAT WORKS AND WHAT DOESN'T

Not only can you get a view of their business operations, you can also evaluate what they are doing right and what they are doing wrong. Your more successful competitors have figured out what works best, and your less successful competitors can provide you with useful examples of what not to do. For instance, you can measure the engagement of the content on your competitors' blog based on the number of social media shares each article has. You might then come up with your own topics based on what worked and what didn't work for your competitor but do it even better.

If your competitors have spent a lot of money optimizing their strategy and development, so much the better! You can reap the benefits of those investments for free with competitor analysis. Cameron Herold, founder of three one-hundred-million-dollar companies (including 1-800-GOT-JUNK), and author of *Double Double*, used this strategy to grow his companies rapidly. He explains his strategy: "To figure out how to do each of the projects that we'd need to grow, I would use R&D, which stood for Rip off & Duplicate. So many great companies have already figured it all out; I'd just figure out who they were and do what they'd done before me."

The Influence of Military Strategies to Business

POSITION YOURSELF TO OUTPERFORM YOUR COMPETITORS ONLINE

Once you know your competitor's strategy, and what they are doing well or poorly, you can craft a winning website redesign strategy to blow them out of the water. This is the ultimate goal of competitor analysis—to give your own website a strategic roadmap to success. At Intechnic, we take the Rip off & Duplicate strategy one step further — "Rip Off, Duplicate, and improve." Instead of simply copying successful ideas, we dissect them to understand not just that they work well, but also why they work well. Then, we customize them to our own business needs. We look at this as a chance for us to create a better strategic plan based on our knowledge of what works.

BEAT YOUR COMPETITORS BEFORE THEY BEAT YOU

Competitive analysis is a two-way street, and what could benefit your company could also work against you. A company's entire website strategy is on display for anyone to assess— and that goes for your website, too. By doing a competitor analysis, you will position yourself to dominate your competitors before they get ahead. One danger of not doing a competitive analysis is that if you aren't actively assessing your competitions' actions, you can be sure that at least one of your competitors will find an opportunity to outdo you. If you go through this exercise, however, you'll learn more about how your competitors think and be able to respond to their tactics proactively.

7 POWERFUL LESSONS SUN TZU CAN
TEACH YOU ABOUT STRATEGY

Sun Tzu Lesson One

S trategy without tactics is the slowest route to victory.
Tactics without strategy is the noise before defeat.

Before thinking – How can my business use Facbook, or "X popular social network" (or any tactic for that matter) step back and ensure that your overall strategy is defined. Do you know how you plan on winning in your respective marketplace? There are two fundamental strategies to consider – low cost or differentiation (Niche).

Low cost is self-explanatory and is the strategy utilized by companies like Wal-Mart or Southwest. If this is your strategy, every tactic you utilize or move you make should fall in line with increasing your customer volume and decreasing your costs. **This could involve tactics like:**

Developing systems to streamline operations Harnessing the power of economies of scale (buying in volume) Economies of scope (lowering costs by spreading risk across various product lines)

Lowering the cost of acquiring a new customer through conversion optimization

Typically, a low-cost strategy is focused on reaching customers broader in nature.

A differentiation strategy focuses on meeting a specific market's needs well. Typically, if you can develop a true competitive advantage that clearly differentiates you from your competitors or alternative solutions in your respective marketplace, your customers will often be willing to pay a premium for your offering.

Differentiation and developing a sustainable competitive advantage is the goal of many firms, but it isn't easy.

A fundamental foundation of strategy is research. How can you form a strategy without being informed?

This brings us to Sun Tzu strategy lesson two.

Sun Tzu Lesson Two

"If you know the enemy and know yourself, you need not fear the result of a hundred battles."

This lesson essentially focuses on understanding your strengths and weaknesses, and those of your competitors. The full Sun Tzu quote is actually… "If you know the enemy and know yourself, you need not fear the result of a hundred battles. If you know yourself but not the enemy, for every victory gained you will also suffer a defeat. If you know neither the enemy nor yourself, you will succumb in every battle."

Start by understanding the strengths and weaknesses of both you and your key competitors. Consider conducting a SWOT analysis to assist you in this endeavor.

In a SWOT analysis, outside of strengths and weaknesses there are also opportunities and threats. Opportunities and Threats are elements occurring outside of a particular company that could affect it.

To understand opportunities and threats, you must have a finger on the pulse of what is occurring in your industry. This takes us to Sun Tzu strategy lesson number three.

Sun Tzu Strategy Lesson Three

"The natural formation of the country is the soldier's best ally."

In this particular quote, Sun Tzu is referencing the terrain or landscape, that one faces in battle. Remember to become very accustomed to the landscape of our industry. We must also be aware of changes that occur in our industry that could affect our business. Change or movement in your industry can create opportunities or threats for you or your competitors. What changes could affect your industry? Here are a few...

New laws or government regulations Disruptive technologies

Changes in the budget of your customers' Social changes and movements

Some industries are more volatile than others, but eventually, change will come. It all comes down to how prepared you are to take advantage of that change.

Sun Tzu Strategy Lesson Four

"The general who wins the battle makes many calculations in his temple before the battle is fought. The general who loses makes but few calculations beforehand."

In this lesson, Sun Tzu expressed that those who prepare in advance by creating well-founded plans are more likely to succeed. There are only twenty-four hours in a day, and there are always excuses that can be made, but those who are successful have invested time into proper planning.

When planning, consider exploring a variety of tactical combinations based on what has worked in the past for you, others in your industry, or even other companies in different industries.

Sun Tzu Strategy Lesson Five

"There are not more than five musical notes, yet the combinations of these five give rise to more melodies than can ever be heard."

Consider planning to utilize conversion optimization by experimenting in A/B testing and multi-variant testing. Plan to test different:

Headlines

Marketing messages

Page layouts

Images

Call to action buttons

Advertisements

Traffic Sources

Keywords

Sun Tzu believed in this concept so much he gave additional examples…

"There are not more than five primary colors, yet in combination they produce more hues than can ever been seen."

"There are not more than five cardinal tastes, yet combinations of them yield more flavors than can ever be tasted."

But to be successful relying solely on planning and strategy isn't enough. Remember what Sun Tzu mentioned in lesson one…

"Strategy before tactics is the slowest route to victory."

A well-founded strategy is only as viable as the ability for a firm to execute and see it through.

Fundamentally, a successful operation comes down to the correct thing happening at the right time.

"The quality of decision is like the well-timed swoop of a falcon which enables it to strike and destroy its victim."

A decision to act only will be successful if the action is appropriate for the situation presented. Having a quality strategy is very important, but recognizing the moment to strike and execute various aspects of your strategy is a very important skill.

This takes practice and requires you to be attuned to what is occurring in your respective marketplace.

The good thing is that as you continue to practice and this valuable skill, you'll notice that the law of attraction will kick in. More opportunities will come your way.

"Opportunities multiply as they are seized."

Success breeds success. In *Thinking in Systems* by Donella H.

Meadows, the author explains a system trap called **"Success to Successful."** Essentially, this, from a systems thinking standpoint, is a flaw where those in a particular competitive environment acquire additional resources as a result of winning that helps them to further compete more effectively in the future.

For example: If a manufacturing firm wins a very large contract, they will bring in additional revenue that could allow them to expand their manufacturing capabilities. Through this expansion, they can produce their products at a more economical rate and higher volume to win future jobs.

Think about how you or your company can take advantage of the "Success to Successful" systems flaw and attract more opportunities and wins.

Through the **"Success to Successful"** concept, more opportunities will continue to come your way. The key, as the great legendary

Coach John Wooden said, is to be balanced and prepared to recognize and take advantage of the various opportunities that come your way.

One final lesson that Sun Tzu mentioned, which may be the most important is that…

"You have to believe in yourself."

PRAISE FOR THE INFLUENCE OF MILITARY STRATEGIES TO BUSINESS

"I like this book, because I'm always doing business, and life is war. You can immediately see the philosophy of a study sharpened on the wet stone of a life led by a soldier in the writing. A good man in the trenches is an asset in the office, and MD White is a valuable one. Leading from a sound historical education on the art of war, and guiding the reader by a solid narrative, this is a book for a new generation of forward thinking business men and women to strengthen their concepts of what they will build tomorrow. "

— Josh Sheets, Author of Retro Horror Brain Candy Novels Blood Night And The Follower

"I was at first, reluctant to review this book as it is outside of my area of knowledge! My life was never in business but, the military and manufacturing. Basically I was the grunt in the trenches. So the one word that caught my eye was Military! I thought ok this should if nothing else be interesting, so I whipped out my schedule and shuffled some things around. Yes as I your book I pulled out my overall war plan and saw some advantages to moving this book forward. So now for a review:

For the first time there is a book on business that a military person can understand! This book is clear and concise in drawing parallels between going to war, and starting up a new business. This is clearly defined by using Sun Tzu's Art of War and good business strategies. The parallels are amazingly similar in both war and business, and certainly not to be overlooked. For the first time in fifty years, I understood what the Author was writing about!"

— D HUNT BETA AND PROOFREADING

"I just want to say there are so many strategies out here in this world on how to prepare for the good and bad in the business world. But MD White said it best and the comparison with the art of war plus strategies based on Military processes, training and knowledge is so captivating and encouraging to make you go back and critique your strategies as a business owner.

If you are a business owner, your personal bookkeeping or contemplating to be a future business owner I recommend that this book is utilized not just read but implemented in your day to day running of your business. There is great food to eat concerning your business, if you don't believe me read this book. This is an awesome read and I pray that it goes far, I pray that you understand what the author was aiming at.

To make your business better make the purchase now, put it in the library and put it on your bookshelf: it's worth it. Your business depends on it!

— ELEASE DOBBS, AUTHOR OF THE FRESH DEW SERIES AND WOMEN'S WORKBOOK

"This book touches on many of the important aspects of running a business (as well as leading a company) and makes the parallels between them and military strategies. Many of the military concepts in this book come from Sun Tzu's famous work, but M.D. White also touches on some other aspects of warfare. He equates the strategies found in military doctrine to business planning, business models, market analysis, strategies for large and small companies, selling strategies, innovation, and more. By approaching the marketplace as your battleground/environment, your competitors as your enemy, and market research as intelligence gathering, it is easy to see how companies are able to apply the multitude of military strategies to their advantage.

As a military officer, I absolutely love the idea of equating military strategies to business practices. What many people forget is that, when you get down to it, a nation's armed forces are a business as well. I love the concept that researching timeless texts could potentially give rise to revolutionary developments in the field of business. I really enjoyed that White was able not only to make the comparisons between warfare and business but also give relevant examples of real-life companies' successes (and failures) based on the concepts presented. It brings the ideas that White is proposing down to the working level and makes them a reality for the reader. What I liked the most about this book was the particular chapters on offensive and defensive strategies. It was extremely interesting for me to see these particular concepts of warfare (e.g. shock and awe, flanking attack, strategic withdraw, etc) applied to a particular commercial sales approach."

— ONLINE BOOK CLUB REVIEW

ABOUT THE AUTHOR

 M.D. White is a serial entrepreneur with empirical knowledge in nearly every industry and sector. His humble beginnings began as a minor with two unlicensed, and very successful, computer companies providing building, programming, and networking services to commercial and individual users, respectively. With age, his ambitions and achievements have only grown. Today he consults for growing ventures, and spends much of his time studying the "psychology of things," a term he coined to describe how and why things work. He is from Stockton, California.

CPSIA information can be obtained
at www.ICGtesting.com
Printed in the USA
BVHW042112190121
598200BV00026B/284